delicious
desserts

delicious desserts

sweet sensations for every occasion

rosemary wilkinson

HERMES HOUSE

This edition published by Hermes House in 2002

© Anness Publishing Limited 1998, 2002

Hermes House is an imprint of
Anness Publishing Limited
Hermes House
88–89 Blackfriars Road
London SE1 8HA

A CIP catalogue record for this book is available from the British Library.

Publisher: Joanna Lorenz
Copy Editor: Karen Douthwaite
Designers: Bill Mason, Siân Keogh

Recipes: Carla Capalbo, Francis Cleary, Deh-Ta Hsiung, Norma MacMillan,
Laura Washburn and Stephen Wheeler
Photographers: Karl Adamson, Edward Allwright, Steve Baxter, James Duncan,
Amanda Heywood, Don Last and Michael Michaels
Food for photography: Carla Capalbo, Francis Cleary, Carole Handslip, Jane Hartshorn,
Wendy Lee, Jane Stevenson and Elizabeth Wolf-Cohen
Stylists: Carla Capalbo, Madeleine Brehaut, Diana Civil, Amanda Heywood, Maria Kelly,
Blake Minton, Kirsty Rawlings and Fiona Tillett
Production Controller: Joanna King

1 3 5 7 9 10 8 6 4 2

Front cover shows Chocolate and Orange Scotch Pancakes, for recipe see page 31

Previously published as *Simply Desserts*

NOTES
For all recipes, quantities are given in both metric and imperial measures and, where appropriate,
measures are given in standard cups and spoons. Follow one set, but not a mixture, because they
are not interchangeable.

Standard spoon and cup measurements are level.
1 tsp = 5ml; 1 tbsp = 15ml; 1 cup = 250ml/8fl oz

Australian standard tablespoons are 20ml. Australian readers should use 3 tsp in place of 1 tbsp
for measuring small quantities of gelatine, cornflour, salt etc.

Medium eggs should be used unless otherwise stated.

CONTENTS

Introduction

Dessert is the crowning glory of any meal – whether family supper or a formal dinner party. It always provides an opportunity for the cook to show off her skills and for everyone to be a little self-indulgent. This superb collection of recipes ranges from light-as-air mousses to substantial hot puddings and from wickedly rich cakes to palate-cleansing fruit confections. There are even low-calorie recipes for sweet-toothed weight-watchers. What they all have in common – apart from being deliciously tempting – is the ease with which they can be prepared. Many of them take only minutes and even so-called difficult dishes, such as soufflés, are made easy by the step-by-step instructions and photographs showing the key stages.

The many traditional classics include Queen of Puddings, Peach Cobbler, Poached Pears in Red Wine, Summer Pudding and Chocolate Chiffon Pie, but there are also some more unfamiliar recipes that will soon become family favourites, such as Watermelon Sherbet, Chocolate Crêpes with Plums and Port, Fruit Kebabs with Mango and Yogurt Sauce and Marbled Swiss Roll. The book is divided into five chapters: Cold Desserts, Hot Puddings, Low Calorie, Fruit Desserts and Cakes, Pies & Tarts. A useful introductory section explains some basic techniques and includes recipes for different kinds of pastry. Helpful hints and tips throughout the book provide further advice and information. Success is virtually guaranteed, every time.

Most of the recipes are based on a family of four people, but they can easily be halved for two or doubled for eight. Whether you are tempted by a melt-in-the-mouth soufflé or a sumptuous cheesecake, you can be sure to find the right dessert for any occasion.

Making Shortcrust Pastry

A meltingly short, crumbly pastry sets off any filling to perfection, whether sweet or savoury. The fat content of the pastry dough can be made up of half butter or margarine and half white vegetable fat or with all one kind of fat.

INGREDIENTS

For a 23cm/9in pastry case
225g/8oz/2 cups plain flour
1.5ml/¼ tsp salt
115g/4oz/8 tbsp fat, chilled and diced

1 Sift the flour and salt into a bowl. Add the fat. Rub it into the flour with your fingertips until the mixture is crumbly.

2 Sprinkle 45ml/3 tbsp iced water over the mixture. With a fork, toss gently to mix and moisten it.

3 Press the dough into a ball. If it is too dry to hold together, gradually add another 15ml/1 tbsp iced water.

4 Wrap the ball of dough with clear film or greaseproof paper and chill it for at least 30 minutes.

5 To make pastry in a food processor: combine the flour, salt and cubed fat in the work bowl. Process, turning the machine on and off, just until the mixture is crumbly. Add 45–60ml/3–4 tbsp iced water and process again briefly – just until the dough starts to pull away from the sides of the bowl. It should still look crumbly. Remove the dough from the processor and gather it into a ball. Wrap and chill.

SHORTCRUST PASTRY VARIATIONS

For Nut Shortcrust
Add 30g/1oz/¼ cup finely chopped walnuts or pecan nuts to the flour mixture.

For Rich Shortcrust
Use 225g/8oz/2 cups flour and 175g/6oz/¾ cup fat (preferably all butter), plus 15ml/1 tbsp caster sugar if making a sweet pie. Bind with 1 egg yolk and 30–45ml/ 2–3 tbsp water.

For a Two-crust Pie
Increase the proportions for these pastries by 50%, thus the amounts needed for basic shortcrust pastry are: 340g/12oz/3 cups flour, 2.5ml/½ tsp salt, 175g/6oz/¾ cup fat, 75–90ml/5–6 tbsp water.

PASTRY MAKING TIPS

It helps if the fat is cold and firm, particularly if making the dough in a food processor. Cold fat has less chance of warming and softening too much when it is being rubbed into the flour, resulting in an oily pastry. Use block margarine rather than the soft tub-type for the same reason.

When rubbing the fat into the flour, if it begins to soften and feel oily, put the bowl in the fridge to chill for 20–30 minutes. Then continue to make the dough.

Liquids used should be ice-cold so that they will not soften or melt the fat.

Take care when adding the water: start with the smaller amount (added all at once, not in a dribble), and add more only if the mixture will not come together into a dough. Too much water will make the dough difficult to handle and will result in tough pastry.

When gathering the mixture together into a ball of dough, handle it as little as possible: overworked dough will again produce a tough pastry.

To avoid shrinkage, chill the pastry dough before rolling out and baking. This 'resting time' will allow any elasticity developed during mixing to relax.

Making French Flan Pastry

The pastry for tarts and flans is made with butter or margarine, giving a rich and crumbly result. The more fat used, the richer the pastry will be – almost like a biscuit dough – and the harder to roll out. If you have difficulty rolling it, you can press it into the tin instead, or roll it out between sheets of clear film. Flan pastry, like shortcrust, can be made by hand or in a food processor. Tips for making, handling and using shortcrust pastry apply equally to this type of pastry.

INGREDIENTS

For a 23cm/9in flan case

200g/7oz/1¾ cups plain flour

2.5ml/½ tsp salt

115g/4oz/½ cup butter or margarine, chilled

1 egg yolk

1.5ml/¼ tsp lemon juice

1 Sift the flour and salt into a bowl. Add the butter or margarine. Rub into the flour until the mixture resembles fine breadcrumbs.

2 In a small bowl, mix the egg yolk, lemon juice and 30ml/ 2 tbsp iced water. Add to the flour mixture. With a fork, toss gently to mix and moisten.

3 Press the dough into a rough ball. If it is too dry to come together, add 15ml/1 tbsp more water. Turn on to the work surface or a pastry board.

4 With the heel of your hand, push small portions of dough away from you, smearing them on the surface.

5 Continue mixing the dough in this way until it feels pliable and can easily be peeled off the work surface or pastry board.

6 Press the dough into a smooth ball. Wrap in clear film and chill for at least 30 minutes.

FLAN PASTRY VARIATIONS

For Sweet Flan Pastry
Reduce the amount of salt to 1.5ml/¼ tsp, add 15ml/1 tbsp caster sugar with the flour.

For Rich Flan Pastry
Use 200g/7oz/1¾ cups flour, 2.5ml/½ tsp salt, 150g/5oz/10 tbsp butter, 2 egg yolks and 15–30ml/ 1–2 tbsp water.

For Rich Sweet Flan Pastry
Make rich flan pastry, adding 45ml/3 tbsp caster sugar with the flour and, if liked, 2.5ml/½ tsp vanilla essence with the egg yolks.

Preparing Fresh Fruit

PEELING AND TRIMMING FRUIT

Citrus Fruit

To peel completely: cut a slice from the top and from the base. Set the fruit base down on a work surface. Using a small sharp knife, cut off the peel lengthways in thick strips. Remove the coloured rind and all the white pith (which has a bitter taste). Cut, following the curve of the fruit.

To remove rind: use a vegetable peeler to shave off the rind in wide strips, taking none of the white pith. Use these strips whole or cut them into fine shreds with a sharp knife, according to recipe directions. Or rub the fruit against the fine holes of a metal grater, turning the fruit so you take just the coloured rind and not the white pith. Or use a special tool, called a citrus zester, to take fine threads of rind. (Finely chop the threads as an alternative method to grating.)

Kiwi fruit

Follow the citrus fruit technique, taking off the peel in thin lengthways strips.

Apples, pears, quinces, mangoes, papayas

Use a small sharp knife or a vegetable peeler. Take off the peel in long strips, as thinly as possible.

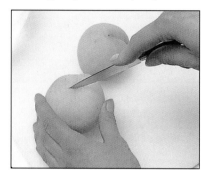

Peaches, apricots

Cut a cross in the base. Immerse the fruit in boiling water. Leave for 10–30 seconds (according to ripeness), then drain and immerse in iced water. The skin should slip off easily.

Pineapple

Cut off the leafy crown. Cut a slice from the base and set the pineapple upright. With a sharp knife, cut off the peel lengthways, cutting thickly to remove the brown "eyes" with it.

Bananas, lychees, avocados

Make a small cut and remove the peel with your fingers or a knife.

Passion fruit, pomegranates

Cut in half, or cut a slice off the top. With a spoon, scoop the flesh and seeds into a bowl.

Star fruit (carambola)

Trim off the tough, darkened edges of the five segments.

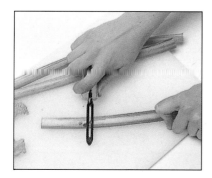

Rhubarb
Cut off the leaves and discard them (they are poisonous). Peel off any tough skin.

Fresh currants (red, black, white)
Pull each cluster through the prongs of a fork to remove the currants from the stalks.

Fresh dates
Squeeze gently at the stalk end to remove the rather tough skin.

CORING AND STONING OR SEEDING FRUIT

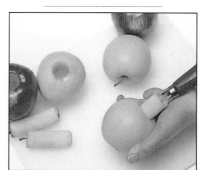

Apples, pears, quinces
For whole fruit: use an apple corer to stamp out the whole core from stalk end to base. Alternatively, working up from the base, use a melon baller to cut out the core. Leave the stalk end intact.

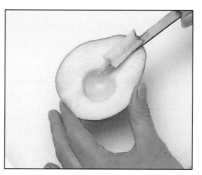

For halves: use a melon baller to scoop out the core. Cut out the stalk and base using a small sharp knife.
For quarters: cut out the stalk and core with a serrated knife.

Citrus fruit
With the tip of a pointed knife, nick out pips from slices or segments.

Cherries
Use a cherry stoner to achieve the neatest results.

Peaches, apricots, nectarines, plums
Cut the fruit in half, cutting round the indentation. Twist the halves apart. Lift out the stone, or lever it out with the tip of a sharp knife.

Fresh dates
Cut the fruit lengthways in half and lift out the stone. Or, if the fruit is to be used whole, cut in from the stalk end with a thin-bladed knife to loosen the stone, then remove it.

Mangoes

Cut lengthways on either side of the large flat stone in the centre. Curve the cut slightly to follow the shape of the stone. Cut the flesh from the two thin ends of the stone.

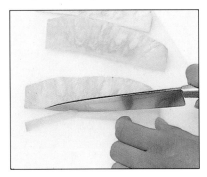

Papayas, melons

Cut the fruit in half. Scoop out the seeds from the central hollow, then scrape away any fibres.

Pineapple

For spears and wedges: cut out the core neatly with a sharp knife.
For rings: cut out the core with a small pastry cutter.

Gooseberries

Use scissors to trim off the stalk and flower ends.

Grapes

Cut the fruit lengthways in half. Use a small knife to nick out the pips. Alternatively, use the curved end of a sterilized hair grip.

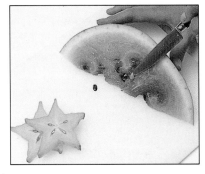

Star fruit (carambola), watermelon

With the tip of a pointed knife, nick out pips from slices.

Strawberries

Use a special huller to remove leafy green top and central core. Or cut these out with a small sharp knife.

Avocado

Cut the fruit in half lengthways. Stick the tip of a sharp knife into the stone and lever it out without damaging the surrounding flesh.

Apples, quinces

For rings: remove the core and seeds with an apple corer. Set the fruit on its side and cut across into thick or thin rings, as required.

For slices: cut the fruit in half and remove core and seeds with a melon baller. Set one half cut side down and cut it across into neat slices, thick or thin according to recipe directions. Or cut the fruit into quarters and remove core and seeds with a knife. Cut lengthways into neat slices.

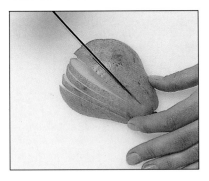

Pears

For fans: cut the fruit in half and remove the core and seeds with a melon baller. Set one half cut side down and cut lengthways into thin slices, not cutting all the way through at the stalk end. Gently fan out the slices so they are overlapping each other evenly. Transfer the pear fan to plate or pastry case using a palette knife.
For slices: follow apple technique.

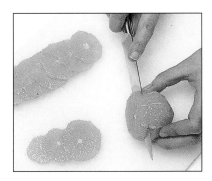

Citrus fruit

For slices: using a serrated knife, cut the fruit across into neat slices.

For segments: hold the peeled fruit in your cupped palm, over a bowl to catch the juice. Working from the side of the fruit to the centre, slide the knife down one side of a separating membrane to free the flesh from it. Then slide the knife down the other side of that segment to free it from the membrane there. Drop the segment into the bowl. Continue cutting out the segments, folding back the membrane like the pages of a book as you work. When all the segments have been cut out, squeeze all the juice from the membrane.

Peaches, nectarines, apricots, plums

For slices: follow apple technique.

Papayas, avocados

For slices: follow apple technique. Or cut the unpeeled fruit into wedges, removing the central seeds or stone. Set each wedge peel side down and slide the knife down the length to cut the flesh away from the peel.
For fans: follow pear technique.

Melon

For slices: follow papaya technique.
For balls: Use a melon baller.

Mangoes

Cut the peeled flesh into slices or cubes, according to recipe directions.

Pineapple

For spears: cut the peeled fruit lengthways in half and then into quarters. Cut each quarter into spears and cut out the core.
For chunks: cut the peeled fruit into spears. Remove the core. Cut across each spear into chunks.
For rings: cut the peeled fruit across into slices. Stamp out the central core from each slice using a pastry cutter.

Kiwi fruit, star fruit (carambola)

Cut the fruit across into neat slices; discard the ends.

Banana

Cut the fruit across into neat slices. Or cut in half and then lengthways into quarters.

COLD
DESSERTS

~

Watermelon Sherbet

A pretty pink sherbet that makes a light and refreshing dessert, or that could be served before the main course to cleanse the palate at a grand dinner.

INGREDIENTS

Serves 6

1kg/2¼lb piece watermelon
200g/7oz/1 cup caster sugar
juice of 1 lemon
2 egg whites
mint leaves, to decorate

1 Cut the watermelon in wedges, then cut it away from the rind, cubing the flesh and picking out all the seeds.

2 Purée three-quarters of the flesh in a food processor or blender, but mash the last quarter on a plate – this will give the sherbet more texture.

3 Stir the sugar with the lemon juice and 120ml/4fl oz/½ cup cold water in a saucepan over very low heat until the sugar dissolves and the syrup clears.

4 Mix all the watermelon and the syrup in a large bowl and transfer to a freezer container.

5 Freeze for 1–1½ hours, until the edges begin to set. Beat the mixture, return to the freezer and freeze for a further 1 hour.

6 When the hour is up, whisk the egg whites to soft peaks. Beat the iced mixture again and fold in the egg whites. Return to the freezer for a further 1 hour, then beat once more and freeze firm.

7 Transfer the sherbet from the freezer to the fridge for 20–30 minutes before it is to be served. Serve in scoops, decorated with mint leaves.

Coffee Granita

A granita is a cross between a frozen drink and a flavoured ice, very popular in Italy. The consistency should be slushy, not solid. They can be made at home with the help of a food processor.

INGREDIENTS

Serves 4–5

115g/4oz/½ cup granulated sugar
250ml/8fl oz/1 cup very strong espresso coffee, cooled
whipped cream, to garnish (optional)

1 Heat 475ml/16fl oz/2 cups of water with the sugar over low heat until the sugar dissolves. Bring to the boil. Remove from the heat and allow to cool.

2 Combine the coffee with the sugar syrup. Place in a shallow container or freezer tray, and freeze until solid. Plunge the bottom of the frozen container or tray in very hot water for a few seconds. Turn the frozen mixture out, and chop it into large chunks.

3 Place the mixture in a food processor fitted with a metal blade, and process until it forms small crystals. Spoon into serving glasses and top with whipped cream, if desired. If you do not wish to serve the granita immediately, pour the processed mixture back into a shallow container or ice tray and freeze until serving time. Allow to thaw for a few minutes before serving, or process again.

Lemon Granita

Nothing is more refreshing on a hot summer's day than a cooling lemon granita.

INGREDIENTS

Serves 4–5

115g/4oz/½ cup granulated sugar
grated rind of 1 lemon, scrubbed before grating
juice of 2 large lemons

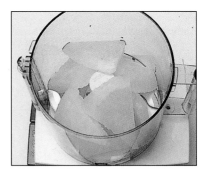

1 Heat 475ml/16fl oz/2 cups of water with the sugar over low heat until the sugar dissolves. Bring to the boil. Remove from the heat, and allow to cool.

2 Combine the lemon rind and juice with the sugar syrup. Place in a shallow container or freezer tray, and freeze until solid.

3 Plunge the bottom of the frozen container or tray in very hot water for a few seconds. Turn the frozen mixture out, and chop it into chunks.

4 Place the mixture in a food processor fitted with a metal blade, and process until it forms small crystals. Spoon into individual serving glasses.

Lime Sherbet

This light, refreshing sherbet is a good dessert to serve after a substantial main course.

INGREDIENTS

Serves 4

250g/9oz/1¼ cups granulated sugar

grated rind of 1 lime

175ml/6fl oz/¾ cup freshly squeezed lime juice

15–30ml/1–2 tbsp fresh lemon juice

icing sugar, to taste

slivers of lime rind, to decorate

1 In a small heavy saucepan, dissolve the granulated sugar in 600ml/1 pint/2½ cups water, without stirring, over medium heat. When the sugar has dissolved, boil for 5–6 minutes. Remove from the heat and let cool.

2 Combine the cooled sugar syrup and lime rind and juice in a measuring jug or bowl. Stir well. Taste and adjust the flavour by adding lemon juice or some icing sugar, if necessary. Do not over-sweeten.

3 Freeze the mixture in an ice-cream maker, following the manufacturer's instructions.

4 If you do not have an ice-cream maker, pour the mixture into a metal or plastic freezer container and freeze until softly set, about 3 hours.

5 Remove from the container and chop roughly into 7.5cm/3in pieces. Place in a food processor and process until smooth. Return the mixture to the freezer container and freeze again until set. Repeat this freezing and chopping process two or three times, until a smooth consistency is obtained.

6 Serve in scoops decorated with slivers of lime rind.

COOK'S TIP

If using an ice-cream maker for these sherbets, check the manufacturer's instructions to find out the freezing capacity. If necessary, halve the recipe quantities.

Chocolate Ice Cream

Use good quality plain or cooking chocolate for the best flavour.

INGREDIENTS

Makes about 900ml/1½ pints/3¾ cups

750ml/1¼ pints/3 cups milk

10cm/4in piece vanilla pod

4 egg yolks

150g/5oz/¾ cup granulated sugar

225g/8oz cooking chocolate, melted

1 To make the custard, heat the milk with the vanilla pod in a small saucepan. Remove from the heat as soon as small bubbles start to form. Do not boil.

2 Beat the egg yolks with a wire whisk or electric beater. Gradually incorporate the sugar, and continue beating for about 5 minutes until the mixture is pale yellow. Strain the milk. Slowly add it to the egg mixture drop by drop.

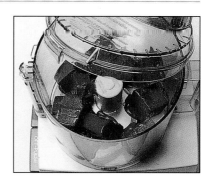

3 Pour the mixture into a double boiler with the melted chocolate. Stir over moderate heat until the water in the pan is boiling, and the custard thickens enough to lightly coat the back of a spoon. Remove from the heat and allow to cool.

4 Freeze in an ice-cream maker, or if you do not have an ice-cream maker, pour the mixture into a metal or plastic freezer container and freeze until set, about 3 hours. Remove from the container and chop roughly into 7.5cm/3in pieces. Place in the bowl of a food processor and process until smooth. Return to the freezer container, and freeze again until firm. Repeat the freezing-chopping process 2 or 3 times, until a smooth consistency is reached.

Boodles Orange Fool

This fool became the speciality of Boodles Club, a gentlemen's club in London's St James's.

INGREDIENTS

Serves 4

4 trifle sponge cakes, cubed

300ml/½ pint/1¼ cups double cream

30–60ml/2–4 tbsp caster sugar

grated rind and juice of 2 oranges

grated rind and juice of 1 lemon

orange and lemon slices and rind,
    to decorate

1 Line the base and halfway up the sides of a large glass serving bowl or china dish with the cubed trifle sponge cakes.

2 Whip the cream with the sugar until it starts to thicken, then gradually whip in the fruit juices, adding the fruit rinds once most of the juices have been incorporated.

3 Carefully pour the cream mixture into the bowl or dish, taking care not to dislodge the sponge. Cover and chill for 3–4 hours. Serve decorated with orange and lemon slices and rind.

Apricot and Orange Jelly

A light and refreshing dessert for a summer's day.

INGREDIENTS

Serves 4

350g/12oz well-flavoured fresh ripe
    apricots, stoned

50–75g/2–3oz/about ⅓ cup
    granulated sugar

about 300ml/½ pint/1¼ cups freshly
    squeezed orange juice

15ml/1 tbsp powdered gelatine

single cream, to serve

finely chopped candied orange peel,
    to decorate

1 Heat the apricots, sugar and 120ml/4fl oz/½ cup of the orange juice, stirring until the sugar has dissolved. Simmer gently until the apricots are tender.

2 Press the apricot mixture through a nylon sieve into a small measuring jug using a spoon.

3 Pour 45ml/3 tbsp of the orange juice into a small heatproof bowl, sprinkle over the gelatine and leave for about 5 minutes, until softened.

4 Place the bowl over a saucepan of hot water and heat until the gelatine has dissolved. Slowly pour into the apricot mixture, stirring all the time. Make up to 600ml/ 1 pint/2½ cups with the remaining orange juice.

5 Pour the apricot mixture into four individual dishes and chill until set. To serve, pour a thin layer of cream over the surface, and decorate with candied orange peel.

Cherry Syllabub

This recipe follows the style of the earliest syllabubs from the sixteenth and seventeenth centuries, producing a frothy, creamy layer over a liquid one.

INGREDIENTS

Serves 4

225g/8oz ripe dark cherries, stoned and chopped

30ml/2 tbsp kirsch

2 egg whites

75g/3oz/scant ½ cup caster sugar

30ml/2 tbsp lemon juice

150ml/¼ pint/⅔ cup sweet white wine

300ml/½ pint/1¼ cups double cream

1 Divide the chopped cherries among six tall dessert glasses and sprinkle over the kirsch.

2 In a clean bowl, whisk the egg whites until stiff. Gently fold in the sugar, lemon juice and wine.

3 In a separate bowl (but using the same whisk), lightly beat the cream then fold into the egg white mixture.

4 Spoon the cream mixture over the cherries, then chill overnight.

Rose Petal Cream

This is an old-fashioned junket which is set with rennet – don't move it while it is setting, otherwise it will separate.

INGREDIENTS

Serves 4

600ml/1 pint/2½ cups milk

45ml/3 tbsp caster sugar

several drops triple-strength rosewater

10ml/2 tsp rennet

60ml/4 tbsp double cream

sugared rose petals, to decorate (optional)

1 Gently heat the milk and 30ml/2 tbsp of the sugar, stirring continuously, until the sugar has melted and the temperature reaches 36.9° C/98.4°F, or the milk feels lukewarm.

2 Stir rosewater to taste into the milk, then remove the pan from the heat before stirring in the rennet.

3 Pour the milk into a serving dish and leave undisturbed for 2–3 hours, until the junket has set.

4 Stir the remaining sugar into the cream, then carefully spoon over the junket. Decorate with sugared rose petals, if you like.

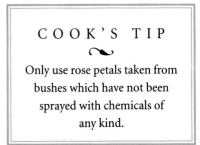

COOK'S TIP

Only use rose petals taken from bushes which have not been sprayed with chemicals of any kind.

Tangerine Trifle

An unusual variation on a traditional trifle — of course, you can add a little alcohol if you wish.

INGREDIENTS

Serves 4

5 trifle sponges, halved lengthways

30ml/2 tbsp apricot jam

15–20 ratafia biscuits

142g/4¾oz packet tangerine jelly

300g/11oz can mandarin oranges, drained, reserving juice

600ml/1 pint/2½ cups ready-made (or home-made) custard

whipped cream and shreds of orange rind, to decorate

caster sugar, for sprinkling

1 Spread the halved sponge cakes with apricot jam and arrange in the base of a deep serving bowl or glass dish. Sprinkle over the ratafia biscuits.

2 Break up the jelly into a heatproof measuring jug, add the juice from the canned mandarins and dissolve in a pan of hot water or in the microwave. Stir until the liquid clears.

3 Make up to 600ml/1 pint/ 2½ cups with ice cold water, stir well and leave to cool for up to 30 minutes. Scatter the mandarin oranges over the cakes and ratafias.

4 Pour the jelly over the mandarin oranges, cake and ratafias and chill for 1 hour.

5 When the jelly has set, pour the custard smoothly over the top and chill again.

6 When ready to serve, pipe the whipped cream over the custard. Wash the orange rind shreds, sprinkle them with caster sugar and use to decorate the trifle.

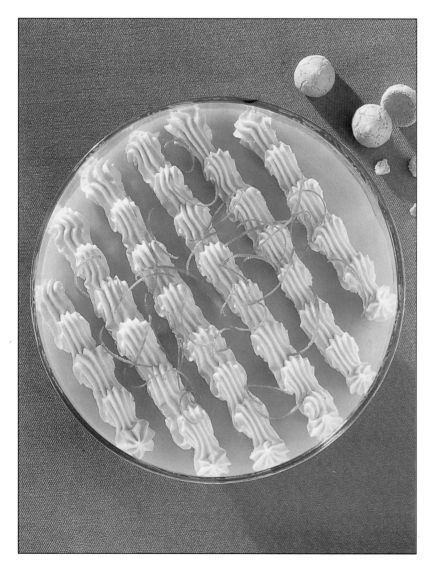

Frozen Strawberry Mousse Cake

Children love this pretty dessert – it tastes just like an ice cream.

Serves 4–6

425g/15oz can strawberries in syrup

15ml/1 tbsp/1 sachet powdered gelatine

6 trifle sponge cakes

45ml/3 tbsp strawberry jam

200ml/7fl oz/⅞ cup crème fraîche

200ml/7fl oz/⅞ cup whipped cream, to decorate

1 Strain the syrup from the strawberries into a large heatproof bowl. Sprinkle over the gelatine and stir well. Stand the bowl in a pan of hot water and stir until the gelatine has dissolved.

2 Leave to cool, then chill for just under 1 hour, until beginning to set. Meanwhile, cut the sponge cakes in half lengthways and spread the cut surfaces with the strawberry jam.

3 Carefully whisk the crème fraîche into the strawberry jelly, then whisk in the canned strawberries. Line a deep, 20cm/8in loose-based cake tin with non-stick baking paper.

4 Pour half the strawberry mousse mixture into the tin, arrange the sponge cakes over the surface, and then spoon over the remaining mousse mixture, pushing down any sponge cakes which rise up.

5 Freeze for 1–2 hours until firm. Remove the cake from the tin and carefully peel away the lining paper. Transfer to a serving plate. Decorate the mousse with whirls of whipped cream and a few strawberry leaves and a fresh strawberry, if you have them.

Gooseberry and Elderflower Cream

When elderflowers are in season, instead of using the cordial, cook two to three elderflower heads with the gooseberries.

INGREDIENTS

Serves 4

500g/1¼lb gooseberries, topped and
   tailed
300ml/½ pint/1¼ cups double cream
about 115g/4oz/1 cup icing sugar, to taste
30ml/2 tbsp elderflower cordial or orange
   flower water (optional)
mint sprigs, to decorate
almond biscuits, to serve

2 Beat the cream until soft peaks form, then fold in half the gooseberries. Sweeten and add elderflower cordial or orange flower water, if using. Sweeten the remaining gooseberries.

3 Layer the cream mixture and the crushed gooseberries in four dessert dishes or tall glasses, then cover and chill. Decorate with mint sprigs and serve accompanied by almond biscuits.

1 Place the gooseberries in a heavy saucepan, cover and cook over a low heat, shaking the pan occasionally, until the gooseberries are tender. Tip the gooseberries into a bowl, crush them, then leave to cool completely.

COOK'S TIP

If preferred, the cooked gooseberries can be puréed and sieved. An equivalent quantity of real custard can replace the cream.

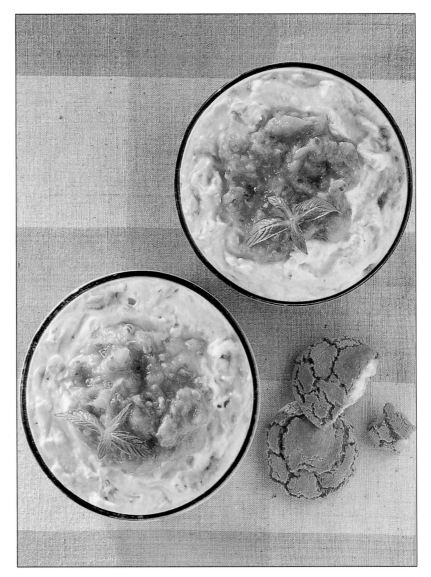

Creole Ambrosia

A refreshing cold fruity pudding that can be made at any time of the year.

INGREDIENTS

Serves 6

6 oranges

1 coconut

25g/1oz/2 tbsp caster sugar

1 Peel the oranges removing all white pith, then slice thinly, picking out seeds with the point of a knife. Do this on a plate to catch the juice.

2 Pierce the "eyes" of the coconut and pour away the milk, then crack open the coconut with a hammer. (This is best done outside on a stone surface.)

COOK'S TIP

~

Mangoes instead of oranges make the dessert more exotic but less authentically Creole.

3 Peel the coconut with a sharp knife, then grate half the flesh coarsely, either on a hand grater or on the grating blade of a blender or food processor.

4 Layer the coconut and orange slices in a glass bowl, starting and finishing with the coconut. After each orange layer, sprinkle on a little sugar and pour over some of the reserved orange juice.

5 Let the dessert stand for 2 hours before serving, either at room temperature or, in hot weather, keep it refrigerated.

White Chocolate Mousse with Dark Sauce

Creamy vanilla-flavoured white chocolate mousse is served with a dark rum and chocolate sauce.

INGREDIENTS

Serves 6–8

200g/7oz white chocolate, broken into squares
2 eggs, separated
60ml/4 tbsp caster sugar
300ml/½ pint/1¼ cups double cream
1 sachet powdered gelatine or alternative
150ml/¼ pint/⅔ cup Greek-style yogurt
10ml/2 tsp vanilla essence

For the sauce

50g/2oz plain chocolate, broken into squares
30ml/2 tbsp dark rum
60ml/4 tbsp single cream

1 Line a 1 litre/1¾ pint/4 cup loaf tin with non-stick baking paper or clear film. Melt the chocolate in a heatproof bowl over hot water, then remove from the heat.

2 Whisk the egg yolks and sugar in a bowl until pale and thick, then beat in the melted chocolate.

3 Heat the cream in a small saucepan until almost boiling, then remove from the heat. Sprinkle the powdered gelatine over, stirring gently until it is completely dissolved.

4 Then pour on to the chocolate mixture, whisking vigorously to mix until smooth.

5 Whisk the yogurt and vanilla essence into the mixture. In a clean, grease-free bowl, whisk the egg whites until stiff, then fold them into the mixture. Tip into the prepared loaf tin, level the surface and chill until set.

6 Make the sauce. Melt the chocolate with the rum and cream in a heatproof bowl over barely simmering water, stirring occasionally, then leave to cool.

7 When the mousse is set, remove it from the tin with the aid of the paper or clear film. Serve in thick slices with the cooled chocolate sauce poured round.

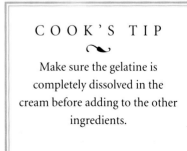

COOK'S TIP

Make sure the gelatine is completely dissolved in the cream before adding to the other ingredients.

Chocolate and Chestnut Pots

Prepared in advance, these are the perfect ending for a dinner party. Remove them from the fridge about 30 minutes before serving, to allow them to "ripen".

INGREDIENTS

Serves 6

250g/9oz plain chocolate

60ml/4 tbsp Madeira

25g/1oz/2 tbsp butter, diced

2 eggs, separated

225g/8oz/scant 1 cup unsweetened
  chestnut purée

crème fraîche or whipped double cream,
  to decorate

1 Make a few chocolate curls for decoration, then break the rest of the chocolate into squares and melt it with the Madeira in a saucepan over a gentle heat. Remove from the heat and add the butter, a few pieces at a time, stirring until melted and smooth.

COOK'S TIP

If Madeira is not available, use brandy or rum instead. These chocolate pots can be frozen successfully for up to 2 months.

2 Beat the egg yolks quickly into the mixture, then beat in the chestnut purée, mixing until smooth.

3 Whisk the egg whites in a clean, grease-free bowl until stiff. Stir about 15ml/1 tbsp of the whites into the chestnut mixture to lighten it, then fold in the rest smoothly and evenly.

4 Spoon the mixture into six small ramekin dishes and chill until set. Serve the pots topped with a generous spoonful of crème fraîche or whipped double cream and decorated with the plain chocolate curls.

HOT
PUDDINGS

~

Chocolate and Orange Scotch Pancakes

Fabulous baby pancakes in a rich creamy orange liqueur sauce.

INGREDIENTS

Serves 4

115g/4oz/1 cup self-raising flour

30ml/2 tbsp cocoa powder

2 eggs

50g/2oz plain chocolate, broken into
   squares

200ml/7fl oz/⅞ cup milk

finely grated rind of 1 orange

30ml/2 tbsp orange juice

butter or oil, for frying

60ml/4 tbsp chocolate curls, for sprinkling

For the sauce

2 large oranges

30ml/2 tbsp unsalted butter

45ml/3 tbsp light muscovado sugar

250ml/8fl oz/1 cup crème fraîche

30ml/2 tbsp Grand Marnier or
   Cointreau

1 Sift the flour and cocoa into a bowl and make a well in the centre. Add the eggs and beat well, gradually incorporating the surrounding dry ingredients to make a smooth batter.

2 Mix the chocolate and milk in a saucepan. Heat gently until the chocolate has melted, then beat into the batter until smooth and bubbly. Stir in the grated orange rind and juice.

3 Heat a large heavy-based frying pan or griddle. Grease with a little butter or oil. Drop large spoonfuls of batter on to the hot surface. Cook over a moderate heat. When the pancakes are lightly browned underneath and bubbly on top, flip them over to cook the other side. Slide on to a plate and keep hot, then make more in the same way.

4 Make the sauce. Grate the rind of 1 of the oranges into a bowl and set aside. Peel both oranges, taking care to remove all the pith, then slice the flesh fairly thinly.

5 Heat the butter and sugar in a wide, shallow pan over a low heat, stirring until the sugar dissolves. Stir in the crème fraîche and heat gently.

6 Add the pancakes and orange slices to the sauce, heat gently for 1–2 minutes, then spoon over the liqueur. Sprinkle with the reserved orange rind. Scatter over the chocolate curls and serve the pancakes at once.

Baked Apples with Caramel Sauce

The creamy caramel sauce turns this simple country dessert into a more sophisticated delicacy.

INGREDIENTS

Serves 6

3 Granny Smith apples, cored but not
   peeled
3 Red Delicious apples, cored but not
   peeled
150g/5oz/¾ cup light brown sugar
2.5ml/½ tsp grated nutmeg
1.5ml/¼ tsp freshly ground black pepper
40g/1½oz/¼ cup walnut pieces
40g/1½oz/scant ¼ cup sultanas
50g/2oz/4 tbsp butter or margarine, diced

For the caramel sauce
15g/½oz/1 tbsp butter or margarine
120ml/4fl oz/½ cup whipping cream

1 Preheat the oven to 190°C/375°F/Gas 5. Grease a baking tin just large enough to hold the apples.

2 With a small knife, cut at an angle to enlarge the core opening at the stem-end of each apple to about 2.5cm/1in in diameter. (The opening should resemble a funnel in shape.)

3 Arrange the apples in the prepared tin, stem-end up.

4 In a small saucepan, combine 175ml/6fl oz/¾ cup of water with the brown sugar, nutmeg and pepper. Bring the mixture to the boil, stirring. Boil for 6 minutes.

5 Mix together the walnuts and sultanas. Spoon some of the walnut-sultana mixture into the opening in each apple.

6 Top each apple with some of the diced butter or margarine.

7 Spoon the brown sugar sauce over and around the apples. Bake, basting occasionally with the sauce, until the apples are just tender, 45–50 minutes. Transfer the apples to a serving dish, reserving the brown sugar sauce in the baking tin. Keep the apples warm.

8 For the caramel sauce, mix the butter or margarine, cream and reserved brown sugar sauce in a saucepan. Bring to the boil, stirring occasionally, and simmer until thickened, about 2 minutes. Leave the sauce to cool slightly before serving.

VARIATION

Use a mixture of firm red and gold pears instead of the apples, preparing them in the same way. Cook for 10 minutes longer.

Queen of Puddings

This hot pudding was developed from a seventeenth-century recipe by Queen Victoria's chefs and named in her honour.

Serves 4

75g/3oz/1½ cups fresh breadcrumbs

60ml/4 tbsp caster sugar, plus 5ml/1 tsp

grated rind of 1 lemon

600ml/1 pint/2½ cups milk

4 eggs

45ml/3 tbsp raspberry jam, warmed

1 Preheat the oven to 160°C/ 325°F/Gas 3. Stir the breadcrumbs, 30ml/2 tbsp of the sugar and the lemon rind together in a bowl. Bring the milk to the boil in a saucepan, then stir into the breadcrumb mixture.

2 Separate three of the eggs and beat the yolks with the whole egg. Stir into the breadcrumb mixture, pour into a buttered baking dish and leave to stand for 30 minutes, then bake the pudding for 50–60 minutes, until set.

COOK'S TIP

Ring the changes by using another flavoured jam, lemon curd, marmalade or fruit purée.

3 Whisk the three egg whites in a large, clean bowl until stiff but not dry, then gradually whisk in the remaining 30ml/2 tbsp caster sugar until the mixture is thick and glossy, taking care not to overwhip.

4 Spread the jam over the pudding, then spoon over the meringue to cover the top completely. Sprinkle the remaining sugar over the meringue, then bake for a further 15 minutes, until the meringue is beginning to turn a light golden colour.

Peach Cobbler

A satisfying pudding which combines fresh peaches with almond-flavoured pastry.

Serves 6

about 1.5kg/3lb peaches, peeled and sliced
45ml/3 tbsp caster sugar
30ml/2 tbsp peach brandy
15ml/1 tbsp fresh lemon juice
15ml/1 tbsp cornflour

For the topping
115g/4oz/1 cup plain flour
7.5ml/1½ tsp baking powder
1.5ml/¼ tsp salt
40g/1½oz/¼ cup finely ground almonds
50g/2oz/¼ cup caster sugar
50g/2oz/4 tbsp butter or margarine
85ml/3fl oz/⅜ cup milk
1.5ml/¼ tsp almond essence

1 Preheat the oven to 220°C/425°F/Gas 7. In a bowl, toss the peaches with the sugar, peach brandy, lemon juice and cornflour, then spoon the peach mixture into a 2 litre/3½ pint/8 cup baking dish.

2 For the topping, sift the flour, baking powder and salt into a mixing bowl. Stir in the ground almonds and all but 1 tablespoon of the sugar. With two knives, or a pastry blender, cut in the butter or margarine until the mixture resembles coarse breadcrumbs.

3 Add the milk and almond essence and stir until the topping mixture is just combined.

4 Drop the topping in spoonfuls on to the peaches. Sprinkle the top with the remaining tablespoon of sugar.

5 Bake until the cobbler topping is browned, 30–35 minutes. Serve hot with ice cream or crème fraîche, if preferred.

Chocolate Crêpes with Plums and Port

A good dinner party dessert, this dish can be made in advance and always looks impressive.

INGREDIENTS

Serves 6

50g/2oz plain chocolate, broken into squares

200ml/7fl oz/⅞ cup milk

120ml/4fl oz/½ cup single cream

30ml/2 tbsp cocoa powder

115g/4oz/1 cup plain flour

2 eggs

For the filling

500g/1¼lb red or golden plums

50g/2oz/¼ cup caster sugar

30ml/2 tbsp port

oil, for frying

175g/6oz/¾ cup crème fraîche

For the sauce

150g/5oz plain chocolate, broken into squares

175ml/6fl oz/¾ cup double cream

30ml/2 tbsp port

1 Place the chocolate in a saucepan with the milk. Heat gently until the chocolate has dissolved. Pour into a blender or food processor and add the cream, cocoa powder, flour and eggs. Process until smooth, then tip into a jug and chill for 30 minutes.

2 Meanwhile, make the filling. Halve and stone the plums. Place them in a saucepan and add the sugar and 30ml/2 tbsp of water. Bring to the boil, then lower the heat, cover, and simmer for about 10 minutes or until the plums are tender. Stir in the port; simmer for a further 30 seconds. Remove the pan from the heat and keep warm.

3 Have ready a sheet of non-stick baking paper. Heat a crêpe pan, grease it lightly with a little oil, then pour in just enough batter to cover the base of the pan, swirling to coat it evenly.

4 Cook until the crêpe has set, then flip it over to cook the other side. Slide the crêpe out on to the sheet of paper, then cook 9–11 more crêpes in the same way.

5 Make the sauce. Combine the chocolate and cream in a saucepan. Heat gently, stirring until smooth. Add the port and heat gently, stirring, for 1 minute.

6 Divide the plum filling between the crêpes, add a dollop of crème fraîche to each and roll them up carefully. Serve in shallow plates, with the chocolate sauce spooned over the top.

Hot Mocha Rum Soufflés

Serve these superb soufflés as soon as they are cooked for a fantastic finale to a dinner party.

INGREDIENTS

Serves 6

25g/1oz/2 tbsp unsalted butter, melted
65g/2½ oz/generous ½ cup cocoa powder
75g/3oz/generous ⅓ cup caster sugar
60ml/4 tbsp strong black coffee
30ml/2 tbsp dark rum
6 egg whites
icing sugar, for dusting

1 Preheat the oven with a baking sheet inside to 190°C/375°F/ Gas 5. Grease six 250ml/8fl oz/ 1 cup soufflé dishes with the melted butter.

2 Mix 15ml/1 tbsp of the cocoa with 15ml/1 tbsp of the caster sugar in a bowl. Tip the mixture into each of the dishes in turn, rotating them so that they are evenly coated.

3 Mix the remaining cocoa with the coffee and rum.

4 Whisk the egg whites in a clean, grease-free bowl until they form firm peaks. Whisk in the remaining caster sugar. Stir a generous spoonful of the whites into the cocoa mixture to lighten it, then gently fold in the remaining whites.

5 Spoon the mixture into the prepared dishes, smoothing the tops. Place on the hot baking sheet, and bake for 12–15 minutes or until well risen. Serve the soufflés immediately, lightly dusted with icing sugar.

COOK'S TIP

When serving the soufflés at the end of a dinner party, prepare them just before the meal is served. Pop in the oven as soon as the main course is finished and serve freshly baked.

Sticky Toffee Pudding

Filling, warming and packed with calories, but still everyone's favourite pudding.

INGREDIENTS

Serves 6

115g/4oz/1 cup toasted walnuts, chopped

175g/6oz/¾ cup butter

175g/6oz/scant 1 cup soft brown sugar

60ml/4 tbsp single cream

30ml/2 tbsp lemon juice

2 eggs, beaten

115g/4oz/1 cup self-raising flour

1 Grease a 900ml/1½ pint/ 3¾ cup pudding basin and add half the walnuts.

2 Heat 50g/2oz/4 tbsp of the butter with 50g/2oz/4 tbsp of the sugar, the cream and 15ml/ 1 tbsp lemon juice in a small pan, stirring until smooth. Pour half into the pudding basin, then swirl to coat it a little way up the sides.

3 Beat the remaining butter and sugar until light and fluffy, then gradually beat in the eggs. Fold in the flour and the remaining nuts and lemon juice and spoon into the bowl.

4 Cover the bowl with grease-proof paper with a pleat folded in the centre, then tie securely with string.

5 Steam the pudding for about 1¼ hours, until it is set in the centre.

6 Just before serving, gently warm the remaining sauce. Unmould the pudding on to a warm plate and pour over the warm sauce.

Chocolate and Orange Soufflé

The base in this soufflé is an easy-to-make semolina mixture, rather than the thick white sauce that most soufflés call for.

INGREDIENTS

Serves 4

600ml/1 pint/2½ cups milk

50g/2oz/generous ⅓ cup semolina

50g/2oz/scant ¼ cup brown sugar

grated rind of 1 orange

90ml/6 tbsp fresh orange juice

3 eggs, separated

65g/2½oz plain chocolate, grated

icing sugar, for sprinkling

1 Preheat the oven to 200°C/400°F/Gas 6. Butter a shallow 1.75 litre/3 pint/7½ cup ovenproof dish.

2 Pour the milk into a heavy-based saucepan, sprinkle over the semolina and brown sugar, then heat, stirring the mixture all the time, until boiling and thickened.

3 Remove the pan from the heat, beat in the orange rind and juice, egg yolks and all but 15ml/ 1 tbsp of the grated chocolate.

4 Whisk the egg whites until stiff, then lightly fold into the semolina mixture in three batches. Spoon into the buttered dish and bake for about 30 minutes, until just set in the centre. Sprinkle with the reserved chocolate and the icing sugar.

Amaretto Soufflé

A mouth-watering soufflé with more than a hint of Amaretto liqueur.

INGREDIENTS

Serves 6

130g/4½oz/½ cup caster sugar

6 amaretti biscuits, coarsely crushed

90ml/6 tbsp Amaretto liqueur

4 eggs, separated, plus 1 egg white

30ml/2 tbsp plain flour

250ml/8fl oz/1 cup milk

pinch of cream of tartar (if needed)

icing sugar, for dusting

1 Preheat the oven to 200°C/ 400°F/Gas 6. Butter a 1.5 litre/ 2½ pint/6¼ cup soufflé dish and sprinkle it with a little of the caster sugar.

2 Put the biscuits in a bowl. Sprinkle them with 30ml/ 2 tbsp of the Amaretto liqueur and set aside.

3 In another bowl, carefully mix the 4 egg yolks, 30ml/ 2 tbsp of the sugar and all the flour.

4 Heat the milk just to the boil in a heavy saucepan. Gradually add the hot milk to the egg mixture, stirring.

5 Pour the mixture back into the pan. Set over a low heat and simmer gently for 3–4 minutes or until thickened, stirring occasionally.

6 Add the remaining Amaretto liqueur. Remove from the heat.

7 In a scrupulously clean, grease-free bowl, whisk the 5 egg whites until they hold soft peaks. (If not using a copper bowl, add the cream of tartar as soon as the whites are frothy.) Add the remaining sugar and continue whisking until stiff.

8 Add about one-quarter of the whites to the liqueur mixture and stir in with a rubber spatula. Add the remaining whites and fold in gently.

9 Spoon half of the mixture into the prepared soufflé dish. Cover with a layer of the moistened amaretti biscuits, then spoon the remaining soufflé mixture on top.

10 Bake for 20 minutes or until the soufflé is risen and lightly browned. Sprinkle with sifted icing sugar and serve immediately.

Chocolate Chip and Banana Pudding

Hot and steamy, this superb light pudding tastes extra special served with chocolate sauce.

INGREDIENTS

Serves 4

200g/7oz/1¾ cups self-raising flour

75g/3oz/6 tbsp unsalted butter or
    margarine

2 ripe bananas

75g/3oz/⅓ cup caster sugar

60ml/4 tbsp milk

1 egg, beaten

60ml/4 tbsp plain chocolate chips or
    chopped chocolate

Glossy Chocolate Sauce and whipped
    cream, to serve

1 Prepare a steamer or half fill a saucepan with water and bring it to the boil. Grease a 1 litre/1¾ pint/4 cup pudding basin. Sift the flour into a bowl and rub in the butter or margarine until the mixture resembles breadcrumbs.

2 Mash the bananas in a bowl. Stir them into the creamed mixture, with the caster sugar.

3 Whisk the milk with the egg in a jug or bowl, then beat into the pudding mixture. Stir in the chocolate chips or chopped chocolate.

4 Spoon the mixture into the prepared basin, cover closely with a double thickness of foil, and steam for 2 hours, topping up the water as required during cooking.

5 Run a knife around the top of the pudding to loosen it, then turn it out on to a warm serving dish. Serve hot, with the chocolate sauce and a spoonful of whipped cream.

COOK'S TIP

If you have a food processor, make a quick-mix version by processing all the ingredients, except the chocolate, until smooth. Stir in the chocolate and proceed as in the recipe.

Steamed Chocolate and Fruit Puddings

Some things always turn out well, including these wonderful little puddings. Dark, fluffy chocolate sponge with tangy cranberries and apple is served with a honeyed chocolate syrup.

INGREDIENTS

Serves 4

115g/4oz/⅔ cup dark muscovado sugar

1 eating apple

75g/3oz/¾ cup cranberries, thawed if frozen

115g/4oz/½ cup soft margarine

2 eggs

75g/3oz/⅔ cup plain flour

2.5ml/½ tsp baking powder

45ml/3 tbsp cocoa powder

For the chocolate syrup

115g/4oz plain chocolate, broken into squares

30ml/2 tbsp clear honey

15ml/1 tbsp unsalted butter

2.5ml/½ tsp vanilla essence

1 Prepare a steamer or half fill a saucepan with water and bring it to the boil. Grease four individual pudding basins and sprinkle each one with a little of the muscovado sugar to coat well all over.

2 Peel and core the apple. Dice it into a bowl, add the cranberries and mix well. Divide equally among the prepared pudding basins.

3 Place the remaining muscovado sugar in a mixing bowl. Add the margarine, eggs, flour, baking powder and cocoa; beat until combined and smooth.

4 Spoon the mixture into the basins and cover each with a double thickness of foil. Steam for about 45 minutes, topping up the boiling water as required, until the puddings are well risen and firm.

5 Make the syrup. Mix the chocolate, honey, butter and vanilla essence in a small saucepan. Heat gently, stirring, until melted and smooth.

6 Run a knife around the edge of each pudding to loosen it, then turn out on to individual plates. Serve at once, with the chocolate syrup.

COOK'S TIP

The puddings can be cooked very quickly in the microwave. Use non-metallic basins and cover with greaseproof paper instead of foil. Cook on High (100% power) for 5–6 minutes, then stand for 2–3 minutes before turning out.

Apple Couscous Pudding

*This unusual couscous mixture
makes a delicious family pudding
with a rich fruity flavour, but
virtually no fat.*

INGREDIENTS

Serves 4

600ml/1 pint/2½ cups apple juice

115g/4oz/⅔ cup couscous

40g/1½oz/scant ¼ cup sultanas

2.5ml/½ tsp mixed spice

1 large Bramley cooking apple, peeled,
    cored and sliced

25g/1oz/2 tbsp demerara sugar

natural low fat yogurt, to serve

1 Preheat the oven to
200°C/400°F/Gas 6. Place the
apple juice, couscous, sultanas and
spice in a pan and bring to the
boil, stirring. Cover and simmer
for 10–12 minutes, until all the free
liquid is absorbed.

COOK'S TIP

To ring the changes, substitute
other dried fruits for the sultanas
in this recipe – try chopped dates
or ready-to-eat pears, figs or
apricots.

2 Spoon half the couscous
mixture into a 1.2 litre/2 pint/
5 cup ovenproof dish and top with
half the apple slices. Top with the
remaining couscous.

3 Arrange the remaining apple
slices overlapping over the top
and sprinkle with demerara sugar.
Bake for 25–30 minutes, or until
the apples are golden brown.
Serve hot with yogurt.

Hot Plum Batter Pudding

Other fruits can be used in place of plums, depending on the season. Canned black cherries are a convenient substitute to keep in the storecupboard.

INGREDIENTS

Serves 4

450g/1lb ripe red plums, quartered and
    stoned
200ml/7fl oz/⅞ cup skimmed milk
60ml/4 tbsp skimmed milk powder
15ml/1 tbsp light muscovado sugar
5ml/1 tsp vanilla essence
75g/3oz/⅔ cup self-raising flour
2 egg whites
icing sugar, to sprinkle

1 Preheat the oven to 220°C/
425°F/Gas 7. Lightly oil a wide, shallow ovenproof dish and add the plums.

2 Pour the milk, milk powder, sugar, vanilla, flour and egg whites into a blender or food processor. Process until smooth.

3 Pour the batter over the plums. Bake for 25–30 minutes, or until puffed and golden. Sprinkle with icing sugar and serve immediately.

COOK'S TIP

If you don't have a food processor, then place the dry ingredients for the batter in a large bowl and gradually whisk in the milk and egg whites.

Glazed Apricot Sponge

Proper puddings can be very high in saturated fat, but this healthy version uses the minimum of oil and no eggs.

INGREDIENTS

Serves 4

10ml/2 tsp golden syrup
411g/14½oz can apricot halves in fruit
    juice
150g/5oz/1¼ cups self-raising flour
75g/3oz/1½ cups fresh breadcrumbs
90g/3½oz/½ cup light muscovado sugar
5ml/1 tsp ground cinnamon
30ml/2 tbsp sunflower oil
175ml/6fl oz/¾ cup skimmed milk

1 Preheat the oven to 180°C/
350°F/Gas 4. Lightly oil a 900ml/1½ pint/3¾ cup pudding basin. Spoon in the syrup.

2 Drain the apricots and reserve the juice. Arrange about 8 halves in the basin. Purée the rest of the apricots with the juice and set aside.

3 Mix the flour, breadcrumbs, sugar and cinnamon then beat in the oil and milk. Spoon into the basin and bake for 50–55 minutes, or until firm and golden. Turn out and serve with the puréed fruit as an accompaniment.

LOW CALORIE

~

Cappuccino Coffee Cups

Coffee-lovers will love this one – and it tastes rich and creamy, even though it's very light.

INGREDIENTS

Serves 4

2 eggs

215g/7.7oz carton evaporated semi-
   skimmed milk

25ml/1½ tbsp instant coffee granules
   or powder

30ml/2 tbsp caster sugar

10ml/2 tsp powdered gelatine,
   or alternative

60ml/4 tbsp light crème fraîche

cocoa powder or ground cinnamon,
   to decorate

1 Separate one egg and reserve the white. Beat the yolk with the whole of the remaining egg.

2 Put the evaporated milk, coffee granules, sugar and beaten eggs in a pan; whisk until evenly combined.

3 Put the pan over a low heat and stir constantly until the mixture is hot, but not boiling. Cook, stirring constantly, without boiling, until the mixture is slightly thickened and smooth.

4 Remove the pan from the heat. Sprinkle the gelatine over the pan and whisk until the gelatine has completely dissolved.

5 Spoon the coffee custard into four individual dishes or glasses and chill them until set.

6 Whisk the reserved egg white until stiff. Whisk in the crème fraîche and then spoon the mixture over the desserts. Sprinkle with cocoa or cinnamon and serve.

VARIATION

Greek-style yogurt can be used instead of the crème fraîche, if you prefer.

Fresh Citrus Jelly

Fresh fruit jellies really are worth the effort – they're packed with fresh flavour, natural colour and vitamins – and they make a lovely fat-free dessert.

INGREDIENTS

Serves 4

3 medium oranges

1 lemon

1 lime

75g/3oz/⅓ cup golden caster sugar

15ml/1 tbsp/1 sachet powdered gelatine, or alternative

extra slices of fruit, to decorate

1 With a sharp knife, cut all the peel and white pith from one orange and carefully remove the segments. Arrange the segments in the base of a 900ml/1½ pint/3¾ cup mould or dish.

2 Remove some shreds of citrus rind with a zester and reserve them for decoration. Grate the remaining rind from the lemon and lime and one orange. Place all the grated rind in a pan, with the sugar and 300ml/½ pint/1¼ cups of water.

3 Heat gently until the sugar has dissolved, without boiling. Remove from the heat. Squeeze the juice from all the rest of the fruit and stir it into the pan.

4 Strain the liquid into a measuring jug to remove the rind (you should have about 600ml/1 pint/2½ cups: if necessary, make up the amount with water). Sprinkle the gelatine over the liquid and stir until it has completely dissolved.

5 Pour a little of the jelly over the orange segments and chill until set. Leave the remaining jelly at room temperature to cool, but do not allow it to set.

6 Pour the remaining cooled jelly into the dish and chill until set. To serve, turn out the jelly and decorate it with the reserved citrus rind shreds and slices of citrus fruit.

Fluffy Banana and Pineapple Mousse

This light, low-fat mousse looks very impressive but is really very easy to make, especially with a food processor. To make it even simpler, use a 1 litre/1¾ pint/4 cup serving dish which will hold all the mixture without a paper "collar".

INGREDIENTS

Serves 6

2 ripe bananas

225g/8oz/1 cup cottage cheese

425g/15oz can pineapple chunks or pieces in juice

15ml/1 tbsp/1 sachet powdered gelatine, or alternative

2 egg whites

1 Tie a double band of non-stick baking paper around a 600ml/ 1 pint/2½ cup soufflé dish, to come 5cm/2in above the rim.

2 Peel and chop one banana and place it in a blender or food processor with the cottage cheese. Process them until smooth.

3 Drain the pineapple, reserving the juice, and reserve a few pieces or chunks for decoration. Add the rest to the mixture in the blender or processor and process for a few seconds until finely chopped.

4 Dissolve the gelatine in 60ml/ 4 tbsp of the reserved pineapple juice. Stir the gelatine quickly into the fruit mixture.

5 Whisk the egg whites until they hold soft peaks and fold them into the mixture. Tip the mousse mixture into the prepared dish, smooth the surface and chill, until set.

6 When the mousse is set, carefully remove the paper collar and decorate with the reserved banana and pineapple.

Summer Fruit Salad Ice Cream

What could be more cooling on a hot day than fresh summer fruits, lightly frozen in this irresistible ice?

INGREDIENTS

Serves 6

900g/2lb/5 cups mixed soft summer fruit, such as raspberries, strawberries, blackcurrants, redcurrants, etc.

2 eggs

225g/8oz/1 cup Greek-style yogurt

175ml/6fl oz/¾ cup red grape juice

15ml/1 tbsp/1 sachet powdered gelatine, or alternative

1 Reserve half the fruit and purée the rest in a blender or food processor, or rub it through a sieve to make a smooth purée.

2 Separate the eggs and whisk the yolks and the yogurt into the fruit purée.

3 Heat the grape juice until it's almost boiling, then remove it from the heat. Sprinkle the gelatine over the juice and stir to dissolve the gelatine completely.

4 Whisk the dissolved gelatine mixture into the fruit purée and then pour the mixture into a freezer container. Freeze until half-frozen and slushy in consistency.

5 Whisk the egg whites until they are stiff. Quickly fold them into the half-frozen mixture.

6 Return to the freezer and freeze until almost firm. Scoop into individual dishes or glasses and add the reserved soft fruits.

Minted Raspberry Bavarois

A sophisticated dessert that can be made a day in advance for a special dinner party.

INGREDIENTS

Serves 6

450g/1lb/2⅔ cups fresh or frozen and
   thawed raspberries
30ml/2 tbsp icing sugar
30ml/2 tbsp lemon juice
15ml/1 tbsp finely chopped fresh mint
30ml/2 tbsp/2 sachets powdered gelatine,
   or alternative
300ml/½ pint/1¼ cups custard, made with
   skimmed milk
250g/9oz/1⅛ cups Greek-style yogurt
fresh mint sprigs, to decorate

1 Reserve a few raspberries for decoration. Place the raspberries, icing sugar and lemon juice in a blender or food processor and process them until smooth.

2 Press the purée through a sieve to remove the raspberry pips. Add the mint. You should have about 600ml/1 pint/2½ cups of purée.

3 Sprinkle 5ml/1 tsp of the gelatine over 30ml/2 tbsp of boiling water and stir until the gelatine has dissolved. Stir into 150ml/¼ pint/⅔ cup of the fruit purée.

4 Pour this jelly into a 1 litre/ 1¾ pint/4 cup mould, and leave the mould to chill in the fridge until the jelly is just on the point of setting. Tip the tin to swirl the setting jelly around the sides, and then leave to chill until the jelly has set completely.

5 Stir the remaining fruit purée into the custard and yogurt. Dissolve the rest of the gelatine in 45ml/3 tbsp of boiling water and stir it in quickly.

6 Pour the raspberry custard into the mould and leave it to chill until it has set completely. To serve, dip the mould quickly into hot water and then turn it out and decorate it with the reserved raspberries and the mint sprigs.

Tofu Berry "Cheesecake"

This summery "cheesecake" is a very light and refreshing finish to any meal. Strictly speaking, it is not a cheesecake at all, as it's based on tofu – but who would guess?

INGREDIENTS

Serves 6

50g/2oz/4 tbsp low-fat spread

30ml/2 tbsp apple juice

115g/4oz/6 cups bran flakes or other high-fibre cereal

For the filling

275g/10oz/1¼ cups tofu or skimmed-milk soft cheese

200g/7oz/⅞ cup low-fat natural yogurt

15ml/1 tbsp/1 sachet powdered gelatine

60ml/4 tbsp apple juice

For the topping

175g/6oz/1¾ cups mixed summer soft fruit, e.g. strawberries, raspberries, red-currants, blackberries, etc. (or frozen "fruits of the forest")

30ml/2 tbsp redcurrant jelly

2 Tip into a 23cm/9in round flan tin and press down firmly. Leave to set.

3 For the filling, place the tofu or cheese and yogurt in a blender or food processor and process them until smooth. Dissolve the gelatine in the apple juice and stir the juice immediately into the tofu mixture.

4 Spread the tofu mixture over the chilled base, smoothing it evenly. Place in the fridge until the filling has set.

1 For the base, place the low-fat spread and apple juice in a pan and heat them gently until the spread has melted. Crush the cereal and stir it into the pan.

5 Remove the flan tin and place the "cheesecake" on a serving plate.

6 Arrange the fruits over the top. Melt the redcurrant jelly with 30ml/2 tbsp hot water. Let it cool, then spoon over the fruit to serve.

COOK'S TIP

The lowest-calorie breakfast cereals are usually those which are highest in fibre, so it is worth checking the labels for comparisons.

Apple Foam with Blackberries

This light dessert provides a good contrast in flavour and colour.

INGREDIENTS

Serves 4

225g/8oz blackberries
150ml/¼ pint/⅔ cup apple juice
5ml/1 tsp powdered gelatine
15ml/1 tbsp clear honey
2 egg whites

1 Place the blackberries in a pan with 60ml/4 tbsp of the apple juice and heat gently until the fruit is soft. Remove from the heat, cool and chill.

2 Sprinkle the gelatine over the remaining apple juice in another pan and stir over a low heat until dissolved. Stir in the honey.

3 Whisk the egg whites in a bowl until they hold stiff peaks. Continue whisking hard and pour in the hot gelatine mixture gradually, until well mixed.

4 Quickly spoon the foam into rough mounds on individual plates. Chill. Serve with the blackberries and juice spooned around.

VARIATION

Any seasonal soft fruit can be used to accompany the apple if blackberries are not available.

COOK'S TIP

Make sure that you dissolve the gelatine over a very low heat. It must not boil, or it will lose its setting ability.

Filo Chiffon Pie

Filo pastry is low in fat and is very easy to use. Keep a pack in the freezer, ready to make impressive puddings like this one.

Serves 3

500g/1¼lb pink rhubarb
5ml/1 tsp mixed spice
finely grated rind and juice of 1 orange
15ml/1 tbsp caster sugar
15g/½oz/1 tbsp butter
3 sheets filo pastry

1 Preheat the oven to 200°C/ 400°F/Gas 6. Trim the leaves and ends from the rhubarb sticks and chop them in 2.5cm/1in pieces. Place them in a bowl.

2 Add the mixed spice, orange rind and juice and sugar and toss well to coat evenly. Tip the rhubarb into a 1 litre/1¾ pint/ 4 cup pie dish.

3 Melt the butter and brush it over the pastry sheets. Lift the pastry sheets on to the pie dish, butter-side up, and crumple them to form a chiffon effect, covering the pie completely.

4 Place the dish on a baking sheet and bake it for 20 minutes, until golden brown. Reduce the heat to 180°C/350°F/ Gas 4 and bake for a further 10–15 minutes, until the rhubarb is tender. Serve warm.

VARIATION

Other fruit such as apples, pears or peaches can be used in this pie – try it with whatever is in season.

Greek Honey and Lemon Cake

The semolina in this recipe gives the cake an excellent texture.

INGREDIENTS

Makes 16 slices

40g/1½oz/3 tbsp sunflower margarine

60ml/4 tbsp clear honey

finely grated rind and juice of 1 lemon

150ml/¼ pint/⅔ cup skimmed milk

150g/5oz/1¼ cups plain flour

7.5ml/1½ tsp baking powder

2.5ml/½ tsp grated nutmeg

50g/2oz/⅓ cup semolina

2 egg whites

10ml/2 tsp sesame seeds

1 Preheat the oven to 200°C/ 400°F/Gas 6. Lightly oil a 19cm/7½in square deep cake tin and line the base with non-stick baking paper.

2 Place the margarine and 45ml/3 tbsp of the honey in a saucepan and heat gently until melted. Reserve 15ml/1 tbsp lemon juice, then stir in the rest with the lemon rind and milk.

3 Stir together the flour, baking powder and nutmeg, then beat in with the semolina. Whisk the egg whites until they form soft peaks, then fold evenly into the semolina mixture.

4 Spoon into the tin and sprinkle with sesame seeds. Bake for 25–30 minutes, until golden brown.

5 Mix the reserved honey and lemon juice and drizzle over the cake while warm. Cool in the tin, then cut into fingers to serve.

Strawberry Roulade

An attractive and delicious cake, perfect for a family supper.

INGREDIENTS

Serves 6

4 egg whites

115g/4oz/scant ⅔ cup golden caster sugar

75g/3oz/⅔ cup plain flour, sifted

30ml/2 tbsp orange juice

caster sugar, for sprinkling

115g/4oz/1 cup strawberries, chopped

150g/5oz/¾ cup low-fat fromage frais

strawberries, to decorate

1 Preheat the oven to 200°C/ 400°F/Gas 6. Oil a 23 x 33cm/ 9 x 13in Swiss roll tin and line with non-stick baking paper.

2 Place the egg whites in a large clean bowl and whisk until they form soft peaks. Gradually whisk in the sugar. Fold in half of the sifted flour, then fold in the rest with the orange juice.

3 Spoon the mixture into the prepared tin, spreading evenly. Bake for 15–18 minutes, or until it is golden brown and firm to the touch.

4 Meanwhile, spread out a sheet of non-stick baking paper and sprinkle with caster sugar. Turn out the cake on to this and remove the lining paper. Roll up the sponge loosely from one short side, with the paper inside. Cool.

5 Unroll and remove the paper. Stir the strawberries into the fromage frais and spread over the sponge. Roll up and serve decorated with strawberries.

FRUIT
DESSERTS

~

Rhubarb-Strawberry Crisp

Strawberries, cinnamon and ground almonds make this a luxurious and delicious version of rhubarb crumble.

INGREDIENTS

Serves 4

225g/8oz strawberries, hulled
450g/1lb rhubarb, diced
90g/3½oz/½ cup granulated sugar
15ml/1 tbsp cornflour
85ml/3fl oz/⅓ cup fresh orange juice
115g/4oz/1 cup plain flour
90g/3½oz/1 cup rolled oats
115g/4oz/½ cup light brown sugar,
   firmly packed
2.5ml/½ tsp ground cinnamon
50g/2oz/½ cup ground almonds
150g/5oz/generous ½ cup cold butter
1 egg, lightly beaten

1 If the strawberries are large, cut them in half. Combine the strawberries, rhubarb and granulated sugar in a 2.4 litre/ 4 pint/10 cup baking dish. Preheat the oven to 180°C/350°F/Gas 4.

2 In a small bowl, blend the cornflour with the orange juice. Pour this mixture over the fruit and stir gently to coat. Set the baking dish aside while making the crumble topping.

3 In a bowl, toss together the flour, oats, brown sugar, cinnamon and ground almonds. With a pastry blender or two knives, cut in the butter until the mixture resembles coarse bread-crumbs. Stir in the beaten egg.

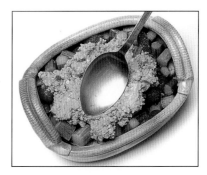

4 Spoon the oat mixture evenly over the fruit and press down gently. Bake until browned, 50–60 minutes, then serve warm.

Fruity Ricotta Creams

Ricotta is an Italian soft cheese with a smooth texture and a mild, slightly sweet flavour. Served here with candied fruit peel and delicious chocolate – it is quite irresistible.

INGREDIENTS

Serves 4

350g/12oz/1½ cups ricotta cheese

30–45ml/2–3 tbsp Cointreau or other orange liqueur

10ml/2 tsp grated lemon rind

30ml/2 tbsp icing sugar

150ml/¼ pint/⅔ cup double cream

150g/5oz/scant 1 cup candied peel, such as orange, lemon and citron, finely chopped

50g/2oz plain chocolate, finely chopped

chocolate curls, to decorate

amaretti biscuits, to serve (optional)

1 Using the back of a wooden spoon, push the ricotta through a fine sieve into a large bowl.

2 Add the liqueur, lemon rind and icing sugar to the ricotta and beat well until the mixture is light and smooth.

3 Whip the cream in a large bowl until it forms soft peaks.

4 Gently fold the cream into the ricotta mixture with the candied peel and chopped chocolate.

5 Spoon the mixture into four glass serving dishes and chill for about 1 hour. Decorate the ricotta creams with chocolate curls and serve with amaretti biscuits, if you like.

Hot Fruit with Maple Butter

Turn exotic fruits into comfort food by grilling them with maple syrup and butter.

INGREDIENTS

Serves 4

1 large mango

1 large paw paw

1 small pineapple

2 bananas

115g/4oz/½ cup unsalted butter

60ml/4 tbsp pure maple syrup

ground cinnamon, for sprinkling

COOK'S TIP
∽

Prepare the fruit just before grilling to prevent it discolouring.

1 Peel the mango and cut the flesh into large pieces. Halve the paw paw and scoop out the seeds. Cut into thick slices, then peel away the skin.

2 Peel and core the pineapple and slice into thin wedges. Peel the bananas then halve them lengthways.

3 Cut the butter into small dice and place in a blender or food processor with the maple syrup, then process until the mixture is smooth and creamy.

4 Place the mango, paw paw, pineapple and banana on a grill rack and brush with the maple syrup butter.

5 Cook the fruit under a medium heat for about 10 minutes, until just tender, turning the fruit occasionally and brushing it with the butter.

6 Arrange the fruit on a warmed serving platter and dot with the remaining butter. Sprinkle over a little ground cinnamon and serve the fruit piping hot.

Ginger Baked Pears

This simple French dessert is the kind that would be served after Sunday lunch or a family supper. Try to find Comice or Anjou pears – this recipe is especially useful for slightly under-ripe fruit.

INGREDIENTS

Serves 4

4 large pears

300ml/½ pint/1¼ cups whipping cream

50g/2oz/¼ cup caster sugar

2.5ml/½ tsp vanilla essence

1.5ml/¼ tsp ground cinnamon

pinch of freshly grated nutmeg

5ml/1 tsp grated fresh root ginger

1 Preheat the oven to 190°C/375°F/Gas 5. Lightly butter a large shallow baking dish.

2 Peel the pears, cut in half lengthways and remove the cores. Arrange, cut side down, in a single layer in the baking dish.

3 Mix together the cream, sugar, vanilla essence, cinnamon, nutmeg and ginger and pour over the pears.

4 Bake for 30–35 minutes, basting from time to time, until the pears are tender and browned on top and the cream is thick and bubbly. Cool slightly before serving.

Prunes Poached in Red Wine

Serve this simple dessert on its own, or with crème fraîche or vanilla ice cream.

INGREDIENTS

Serves 8–10

1 unwaxed orange

1 unwaxed lemon

750ml/1¼ pints/3 cups fruity red wine

50g/2oz/¼ cup caster sugar, or to taste

1 cinnamon stick

pinch of freshly grated nutmeg

2 or 3 cloves

5ml/1 tsp black peppercorns

1 bay leaf

900g/2lb large stoned prunes, soaked in cold water

cream, to serve

strips of orange rind, to decorate

1 Using a vegetable peeler, peel two or three strips of rind from both the orange and lemon. Squeeze the juice from both and put in a large saucepan.

2 Add the wine, sugar, spices, peppercorns, bay leaf, strips of rind to the pan and 475ml/16fl oz/ 2 cups water.

3 Bring to the boil over a medium heat, stirring occasionally to dissolve the sugar. Drain the prunes and add to the saucepan, reduce the heat to low and simmer, covered, for 10–15 minutes until the prunes are tender. Remove from the heat and set aside until cool.

4 Using a slotted spoon, transfer the prunes to a serving dish. Return the cooking liquid to a medium-high heat and bring to the boil. Boil for 5–10 minutes until slightly reduced and syrupy, then pour or strain over the prunes. Cool, then chill before serving with cream, decorated with strips of orange rind, if you like.

Blueberry Pancakes

These are rather like the thick American breakfast pancakes – though they can, of course, be eaten at any time of the day.

INGREDIENTS

Makes 6–8

115g/4oz/1 cup self-raising flour

pinch of salt

45–60ml/3–4 tbsp caster sugar

2 eggs

120ml/4fl oz/½ cup milk

15–30ml/1–2 tbsp oil

115g/4oz/1 cup fresh or frozen
    blueberries, plus extra to decorate

maple syrup, to serve

lemon wedges, to decorate

1 Sift the flour into a bowl with the salt and sugar. Beat together the eggs thoroughly. Make a well in the middle of the flour and stir in the eggs.

2 Gradually blend in a little of the milk to make a smooth batter. Then whisk in the rest of the milk and whisk for 1–2 minutes. Allow to rest for 20–30 minutes.

3 Heat a few drops of oil in a pancake pan or heavy-based frying pan until just hazy. Pour about 30ml/2 tbsp of the batter and swirl the batter around until it makes an even shape.

4 Cook for 2–3 minutes and when almost set on top, sprinkle over 15–30ml/1–2 tbsp blueberries. As soon as the base is loose and golden brown, turn the pancake over.

5 Cook on the second side for only about 1 minute, until golden and crisp. Slide the pancake on to a plate and serve drizzled with maple syrup. Continue with the rest of the batter. Serve decorated with lemon wedges and a few extra blueberries.

COOK'S TIP

Instead of blueberries you could use blackberries or raspberries. If you use canned fruit, make sure it is very well drained.

Chocolate Amaretti Peaches

Quick and easy to prepare, this delicious dessert can also be made with fresh nectarines or apricots.

INGREDIENTS

Serves 4

115g/4oz amaretti biscuits, crushed

50g/2oz plain chocolate, chopped

grated rind of ½ orange

15ml/1 tbsp clear honey

1.5ml/¼ tsp ground cinnamon

1 egg white, lightly beaten

4 firm ripe peaches

150ml/¼ pint/⅔ cup white wine

15ml/1 tbsp caster sugar

whipped cream, to serve

1 Preheat the oven to 190°C/375°F/Gas 5. Mix together the crushed amaretti biscuits, chocolate, orange rind, honey and cinnamon in a bowl. Add the beaten egg white and mix to bind the mixture together.

2 Halve and stone the peaches and fill the cavities with the chocolate mixture, mounding it up slightly.

3 Arrange the stuffed peaches in a lightly buttered, shallow ovenproof dish which will just hold the peaches comfortably. Pour the wine into a measuring cup and stir in the sugar.

4 Pour the wine mixture around the peaches. Bake for 30–40 minutes, until the peaches are tender. Serve at once with a little of the cooking juices spooned over and the whipped cream.

Poached Pears in Red Wine

This makes a very pretty dessert, as the pears take on a red blush from the wine.

INGREDIENTS

Serves 4

1 bottle red wine

150g/5oz/¾ cup caster sugar

45ml/3 tbsp honey

juice of ½ lemon

1 cinnamon stick

1 vanilla pod, split open lengthways

5cm/2in piece of orange rind

1 clove

1 black peppercorn

4 firm, ripe pears

whipped cream or soured cream, to serve

1 Place the wine, sugar, honey, lemon juice, cinnamon stick, vanilla pod, orange rind, clove and peppercorn in a saucepan just large enough to hold the pears standing upright. Heat gently, stirring occasionally until the sugar has completely dissolved.

2 Meanwhile, peel the pears, leaving the stem intact. Take a thin slice off the base of each pear so that it will stand square and upright in the pan.

3 Place the pears in the wine mixture, then simmer, uncovered, for 20–35 minutes depending on size and ripeness, until the pears are just tender; be careful not to overcook.

4 Carefully transfer the pears to a bowl using a slotted spoon. Continue to boil the poaching liquid until reduced by about half. Leave to cool, then strain the cooled liquid over the pears and chill for at least 3 hours.

5 Place the pears in four individual serving dishes and spoon over a little of the red wine syrup. Serve with whipped cream or soured cream.

Raspberry Trifle

Use fresh or frozen raspberries for this ever-popular desert.

INGREDIENTS

Serves 6 or more

175g/6oz trifle sponges or plain Victoria
   sponge, cut into 2.5cm/1in cubes , or
   coarsely crumbled sponge fingers
60ml/4 tbsp medium sherry
115g/4oz raspberry jam
275g/10oz/1⅔ cups raspberries
450ml/¾ pint/scant 2 cups custard,
   flavoured with 30ml/2 tbsp medium or
   sweet sherry
300ml/½ pint/1¼ cups sweetened
   whipped cream
toasted flaked almonds and mint leaves,
   to decorate

1 Spread half of the sponges, cake cubes or sponge fingers over the bottom of a large serving bowl. (A glass bowl is best for presentation.)

2 Sprinkle half of the sherry over the cake to moisten it. Spoon over half of the jam, dotting it evenly over the cake cubes.

3 Reserve a few raspberries for decoration. Make a layer of half of the remaining raspberries on top.

4 Pour over half of the custard, covering the fruit and cake. Repeat the layers. Cover and chill for at least 2 hours.

5 Before serving, spoon the sweetened whipped cream evenly over the top. To decorate, sprinkle with toasted flaked almonds and arrange the reserved raspberries and the mint leaves on the top.

VARIATION

Use other ripe summer fruit such as apricots, peaches, nectarines and strawberries in the trifle, with jam and liqueur to suit.

Fruit Kebabs with Mango and Yogurt Sauce

These mixed fresh fruit kebabs make an attractive and healthy dessert.

INGREDIENTS

Serves 4

½ pineapple, peeled, cored and cubed

2 kiwi fruit, peeled and cubed

175g/6oz/1½ cups strawberries, hulled and cut in half, if large

½ mango, peeled, stoned and cubed

For the sauce

120ml/4fl oz/½ cup fresh mango purée, from 1–1½ peeled and stoned mangoes

120ml/4fl oz/½ cup thick plain yogurt

5ml/1 tsp caster sugar

few drops of vanilla essence

15ml/1 tbsp finely chopped mint leaves

1 To make the sauce, beat together the mango purée, yogurt, sugar and vanilla with an electric mixer.

2 Stir in the chopped mint. Cover the sauce and place in the fridge until required.

3 Thread the prepared fruit on to twelve 15cm/6in wooden skewers, alternating the pineapple, kiwi fruit, strawberries and mango cubes.

4 Arrange the kebabs on a large serving tray with the mango and yogurt sauce in the centre.

Tropical Fruits in Cinnamon Syrup

An exotic glazed fruit salad, a simply prepared but satisfying end to any meal.

INGREDIENTS

Serves 6

450g/1lb/2¼ cups caster sugar

1 cinnamon stick

1 large or 2 medium paw paws (about 675g/1½lb), peeled, seeded and cut lengthways into thin pieces

1 large or 2 medium mangoes (about 675g/1½lb), peeled, stoned and cut lengthways into thin pieces

1 large or 2 small star fruit (about 225g/8oz), thinly sliced

yogurt or crème fraîche, to serve

1 Sprinkle one-third of the sugar over the base of a large saucepan. Add the cinnamon stick and half the paw paw, mango and star fruit pieces.

2 Sprinkle half of the remaining sugar over the fruit pieces in the pan. Add all the remaining fruit and sprinkle with the rest of the sugar.

3 Cover the pan and cook the fruit over a medium-low heat for 35–45 minutes, until the sugar melts completely. Shake the pan occasionally, but do not stir or the fruit will collapse.

4 Uncover the pan and simmer until the fruit begins to appear translucent, about 10 minutes. Remove the pan from the heat and leave to cool.

5 Transfer the fruit and syrup to a bowl, cover and chill overnight. Serve with yogurt or crème fraîche.

Clementines in Cinnamon Caramel

The combination of sweet, yet sharp clementines and caramel sauce with a hint of spice is divine. Served with Greek-style yogurt or crème fraîche, this makes a delicious dessert.

INGREDIENTS

Serves 4–6

8–12 clementines

225g/8oz/generous 1 cup granulated sugar

2 cinnamon sticks

30ml/2 tbsp orange-flavoured liqueur

25g/1oz/¼ cup shelled pistachio nuts

1 Pare the rind from two clementines using a vegetable peeler and cut it into fine strips. Set aside.

2 Peel the clementines, removing all the pith but keeping them intact. Put the fruit in a serving bowl.

3 Gently heat the sugar in a pan until it melts and turns a rich golden brown. Immediately turn off the heat.

4 Cover your hand with a dish towel and pour in 300ml/ ½ pint/1¼ cups warm water (the mixture will bubble and splutter). Bring slowly to the boil, stirring until the caramel has dissolved. Add the shredded peel and cinnamon sticks, then simmer for 5 minutes. Stir in the orange-flavoured liqueur.

5 Leave the syrup to cool for about 10 minutes, then pour over the clementines. Cover the bowl and chill for several hours or overnight.

6 Blanch the pistachio nuts in boiling water. Drain, cool and remove the dark outer skins. Scatter over the clementines and serve at once.

Summer Pudding

Unbelievably simple to make and totally delicious, this is a real warm weather classic.

Serves 4

about 8 thin slices day-old white bread, crusts removed
800g/1¾lb mixed summer fruits
about 30ml/2 tbsp granulated sugar

1 Cut a round from one slice of bread to fit in the base of a 1.2 litre/2 pint/5 cup pudding basin, then cut strips of bread about 5cm/2in wide to line the basin, overlapping the strips.

2 Gently heat the fruit, sugar and 30ml/2 tbsp water in a large heavy saucepan, shaking the pan occasionally, until the juices begin to run.

3 Reserve about 45ml/3 tbsp fruit juice, then spoon the fruit and remaining juice into the basin, taking care not to dislodge the bread lining.

4 Cut the remaining bread to fit entirely over the fruit. Stand the basin on a plate and cover with a saucer or small plate that will just fit inside the top of the basin, Place a heavy weight on top. Chill the pudding and the reserved fruit juice overnight.

5 Run a knife carefully around the inside of the basin rim, then invert the pudding on to a cold serving plate. Pour over the reserved juice and serve.

COOK'S TIP

Summer pudding freezes well so make an extra one to enjoy during the winter.

Ruby Plum Mousse

Red plums and port give this mousse its delicate flavour and colour

INGREDIENTS

Serves 6

450g/1lb ripe red plums
45ml/3 tbsp granulated sugar
60ml/4 tbsp ruby port
15ml/1 tbsp/1 sachet powdered gelatine
3 eggs, separated
115g/4oz/generous ½ cup caster sugar
150ml/¼ pint/⅔ cup double cream
skinned and chopped pistachio nuts, to
    decorate
cinnamon biscuits, to serve (optional)

1 Place the plums and granulated sugar in a pan with 30ml/ 2 tbsp water. Cook over a low heat until softened. Press the fruit through a sieve to remove the stones and skins. Leave to cool, then stir in the port.

2 Put 45ml/3 tbsp water in a small bowl, sprinkle over the gelatine and leave to soften. Stand the bowl in a pan of hot water and leave until dissolved. Stir into the plum purée.

3 Place the egg yolks and caster sugar in a bowl and whisk until thick and mousse-like. Fold in the plum purée, then whip the cream and fold in gently.

4 Whisk the egg whites until they hold stiff peaks, then carefully fold in using a metal spoon. Divide among six glasses and chill until set.

5 Decorate the mousses with chopped pistachio nuts and serve with crisp cinnamon biscuits, if liked.

Warm Autumn Compote

An easily prepared dessert with a sophisticated taste.

INGREDIENTS

Serves 4

75g/3oz/6 tbsp caster sugar
1 bottle red wine
1 vanilla pod, split
1 strip pared lemon rind
4 pears
2 purple figs, quartered
225g/8oz/1⅓ cups raspberries
lemon juice, to taste

1 Put the sugar and wine in a large pan and heat gently until the sugar is dissolved. Add the vanilla pod and lemon rind and bring to the boil, then simmer for 5 minutes.

2 Peel and halve the pears, then scoop out the cores, using a melon baller. Add the pears to the syrup and poach for 15 minutes, turning the pears several times so they colour evenly.

3 Add the figs and poach for a further 5 minutes, until the fruits are tender.

4 Transfer the poached pears and figs to a serving bowl using a slotted spoon, then scatter over the raspberries.

5 Return the syrup to the heat and boil rapidly to reduce slightly and concentrate the flavour. Add a little lemon juice to taste. Strain the syrup over the fruits and serve warm.

Greek Fig and Honey Pudding

A quick and easy pudding made from fresh or canned figs topped with thick and creamy Greek-style yogurt, drizzled with honey and sprinkled with pistachio nuts.

INGREDIENTS

Serves 4

4 fresh or canned figs

2 x 225g/8oz tubs/2 cups Greek-style strained yogurt

60ml/4 tbsp clear honey

30ml/2 tbsp chopped pistachio nuts

1 Chop the figs and place in the bottom of four stemmed wine glasses or deep, individual dessert bowls.

2 Top each glass or bowl of figs with half a tub (½ cup) of the Greek-style yogurt. Chill until ready to serve.

3 Just before serving drizzle 15ml/1 tbsp honey over each one and sprinkle with the pistachio nuts.

COOK'S TIP

~

Try specialist honeys made from clover, acacia or thyme.

Russian Fruit Compote

This fruit pudding is traditionally called "Kissel" and is made from the thickened juice of stewed red- or blackcurrants. This recipe uses the whole fruit with an added dash of blackberry liqueur.

INGREDIENTS

Serves 4

225g/8oz/2 cups red- or blackcurrants or a mixture of both

225g/8oz/1⅓ cups raspberries

50g/2oz/4 tbsp caster sugar

25ml/1½ tbsp arrowroot

15–30ml/1–2 tbsp Crème de Mûre

Greek-style yogurt, to serve

1 Place the red- or blackcurrants, raspberries and sugar in a pan with 150ml/¼ pint/⅔ cup water. Cover the pan and cook gently over a low heat for 12–15 minutes, until the fruit is soft.

2 Blend the arrowroot with a little water in a bowl and stir into the fruit. Bring back to the boil, stirring until thickened.

3 Remove from the heat and cool slightly, then gently stir in the Crème de Mûre.

4 Pour into four serving bowls and leave until cold, then chill. Serve topped with spoonfuls of Greek-style yogurt.

CAKES,
PIES & TARTS
~

Chocolate Layer Cake

The cake layers can be made ahead, wrapped and frozen for future use. Always defrost cakes completely before icing.

INGREDIENTS

Serves 10–12

unsweetened cocoa for dusting

225g/8oz can cooked whole beetroot, drained and juice reserved

115g/4oz/½ cup unsalted butter, softened

500g/1¼lb/2½ cups light brown sugar, firmly packed

3 eggs

15ml/1 tbsp vanilla essence

75g/3oz unsweetened chocolate, melted

275g/10oz/2¼ cups plain flour

10ml/2 tsp baking powder

2.5ml/½ tsp salt

120ml/4fl oz/½ cup buttermilk

chocolate curls (optional)

For the chocolate ganache frosting

475ml/16fl oz/2 cups whipping or double cream

500g/1¼lb fine quality, bittersweet or semi-sweet chocolate, chopped

15ml/1 tbsp vanilla essence

1 Preheat the oven to 180°C/ 350°F/ Gas 4. Grease two 23cm/9in cake tins and dust the bottoms and sides with cocoa. Grate the beetroot and add to the beet juice. With an electric mixer, beat the butter, brown sugar, eggs and vanilla until pale and fluffy (3–5 minutes). Reduce the speed and beat in the chocolate.

2 In a bowl, sift the flour, baking powder and salt. With the mixer on low speed, alternately beat in the flour mixture in fourths and buttermilk in thirds. Add the beets and juice and beat for 1 minute. Divide between the tins and bake for 30–35 minutes or until a cake tester inserted in the centre comes out clean. Cool for 10 minutes, unmould and cool.

3 To make the frosting, in a heavy-based saucepan over medium heat, heat the cream until it just begins to boil, stirring occasionally to prevent it from scorching.

4 Remove from the heat and stir in the chocolate, stirring constantly until melted and smooth. Stir in the vanilla. Strain into a bowl and refrigerate, stirring every 10 minutes, until spreadable, about 1 hour.

5 Assemble the cake. Place one layer on a serving plate and spread with one-third of the ganache. Turn the cake layer bottom side up, top with the second layer and spread the remaining ganache over the top and sides of the cake. If using, top with curls. Allow to set for 20–30 minutes, then refrigerate.

Sponge Cake with Fruit and Cream

Called Génoise, this is the French cake used as the base for both simple and elaborate creations. You could simply dust it with icing sugar, or layer it with seasonal fruits to serve as a seasonal dessert.

INGREDIENTS

Serves 6

115g/4oz/1 cup plain flour

pinch of salt

4 eggs, at room temperature

115g/4oz/scant ⅔ cup caster sugar

2.5ml/½ tsp vanilla essence

50g/2oz/4 tbsp butter, melted or clarified and cooled

For the filling

450g/1lb fresh strawberries or raspberries

30–60ml/2–4 tbsp caster sugar

475ml/16fl oz/2 cups whipping cream

5ml/1 tsp vanilla essence

1 Preheat the oven to 180°C/350°F/Gas 4. Lightly butter a 23cm/9in springform tin or deep cake tin. Line the base with non-stick baking paper, and dust lightly with flour. Sift the flour and salt together twice.

2 Half-fill a medium saucepan with hot water and set over a low heat (do not allow the water to boil). Put the eggs in a heatproof bowl which just fits into the pan without touching the water. Using an electric mixer, beat the eggs at medium-high speed, gradually adding the sugar, for 8–10 minutes until the mixture is very thick and pale and leaves a ribbon trail when the beaters are lifted. Remove the bowl from the pan, add the vanilla essence and continue beating until the mixture is cool.

3 Fold in the flour mixture in three batches, using a balloon whisk or metal spoon. Before the third addition of flour, stir a large spoonful of the mixture into the melted or clarified butter to lighten it, then fold the butter into the remaining mixture with the last addition of flour. Work quickly, but gently, so the mixture does not deflate. Pour into the prepared tin, smoothing the top so the sides are slightly higher than the centre.

4 Bake in the oven for about 25–30 minutes until the top of the cake springs back when touched and the edge begins to shrink away from the sides of the tin. Place the cake in its tin on a wire rack to cool for 5–10 minutes, then invert the cake on to the rack to cool completely. Peel off the baking paper.

5 To make the filling, slice the strawberries, place in a bowl, sprinkle with 15–30ml/1–2 tbsp of the sugar and set aside. Beat the cream with 15–30ml/1–2 tbsp of the sugar and the vanilla essence until it holds soft peaks.

6 To assemble the cake (up to 4 hours before serving), split the cake horizontally, using a serrated knife. Place the top, cut side up, on a serving plate. Spread with a third of the cream and cover with an even layer of sliced strawberries.

7 Place the bottom half of the cake, cut side down, on top of the filling and press lightly. Spread the remaining cream over the top and sides of the cake. Chill until ready to serve. Serve the remaining strawberries with the cake.

Warm Lemon and Syrup Cake

The combination of pears, sticky syrup and lemon makes this a real winner. Drizzle with single cream for extra luxury.

Serves 8

3 eggs

175g/6oz/¾ cup butter, softened

175g/6oz/¾ cup caster sugar

175g/6oz/1½ cups self-raising flour

50g/2oz/½ cup ground almonds

1.5ml/¼ tsp freshly grated nutmeg

50g/2oz/5 tbsp candied lemon peel, finely chopped

grated rind of 1 lemon

30ml/2 tbsp lemon juice

poached pears, to serve

For the syrup

175g/6oz/¾ cup caster sugar

juice of 3 lemons

1 Preheat the oven to 180°C/350°F/Gas 4. Grease and base-line a deep, round 20cm/8in cake tin.

2 Place all the cake ingredients in a large bowl and beat well for 2–3 minutes, until the mixture is light and fluffy.

3 Tip the mixture into the prepared tin, spread level and bake for 1 hour, or until golden and firm to the touch.

4 Meanwhile, make the syrup. Put the sugar, lemon juice and 75ml/5 tbsp water in a pan. Heat gently, stirring until the sugar has dissolved, then boil, without stirring, for 1–2 minutes.

5 Turn out the cake on to a plate with a rim. Prick the surface of the cake all over with a fork, then pour over the hot syrup. Leave to soak for about 30 minutes. Serve the cake warm with thin wedges of poached pears.

Marbled Swiss Roll

Simply sensational – that's the combination of light chocolate sponge and walnut chocolate buttercream.

INGREDIENTS

Serves 6–8

90g/3½oz/scant 1 cup plain flour

15ml/1 tbsp cocoa powder

25g/1oz plain chocolate, grated

25g/1oz white chocolate, grated

3 eggs

115g/4oz/generous ½ cup caster sugar

For the filling

75g/3oz/6 tbsp unsalted butter or
  margarine, softened

175g/6oz/1½ cups icing sugar

15ml/1 tbsp cocoa powder

2.5ml/½ tsp vanilla essence

45ml/3 tbsp chopped walnuts

plain and white chocolate curls, to
  decorate (optional)

1 Preheat the oven to 200°C/400°F/Gas 6. Grease a 30 x 20cm/12 x 8in Swiss roll tin and line with non-stick baking paper. Sift half the flour with the cocoa into a bowl. Stir in the grated plain chocolate. Sift the remaining flour into another bowl; stir in the grated white chocolate.

2 Whisk the eggs and sugar in a heatproof bowl; set over a saucepan of hot water until the mixture holds its shape when the whisk is lifted.

3 Remove the bowl from the heat and tip half the mixture into a separate bowl. Fold the white chocolate mixture into one portion, then fold the plain chocolate mixture into the other. Stir 15ml/1 tbsp boiling water into each half to soften the mixtures.

4 Place alternate spoonfuls of the mixture in the prepared tin and swirl lightly together for a marbled effect. Bake for about 12–15 minutes, or until firm. Turn out on to a sheet of non-stick baking paper.

5 Trim the edges to neaten and cover with a damp, clean dish towel. Cool.

6 For the filling, beat the butter or margarine, icing sugar, cocoa powder and vanilla essence together in a bowl until smooth, then mix in the walnuts.

7 Uncover the sponge, lift off the baking paper and spread the surface with the buttercream. Roll up carefully from a long side and place on a serving plate. Decorate with plain and white chocolate curls, if wished.

Blueberry-Hazelnut Cheesecake

The base for this cheesecake is made with ground hazelnuts – a tasty and unusual alternative to a biscuit base.

Serves 6–8

350g/12oz blueberries

15ml/1 tbsp clear honey

75g/3oz/6 tbsp granulated sugar

juice of 1 lemon

175g/6oz/¾ cup cream cheese, at room temperature

1 egg

5ml/1 tsp hazelnut liqueur (optional)

120ml/4fl oz/½ cup whipping cream

For the base

175g/6oz/1⅔ cups ground hazelnuts

75g/3oz/⅔ cup plain flour

pinch of salt

50g/2oz/4 tbsp butter, at room temperature

65g/2½oz/⅓ cup light brown sugar, firmly packed

1 egg yolk

1 For the base, put the hazelnuts in a large bowl. Sift in the flour and salt, and stir to mix. Set aside.

2 Beat the butter with the brown sugar until light and fluffy. Beat in the egg yolk. Gradually fold in the nut mixture, in three batches, until well combined.

3 Press the dough into a greased 23cm/9in pie tin, spreading it evenly against the sides. Form a rim around the top edge that is slightly thicker than the sides. Cover and chill for at least 30 minutes.

4 Preheat the oven to 180°C/350°F/Gas 4. Meanwhile, for the topping, combine the blueberries, honey, 15ml/1 tbsp of the granulated sugar and 5ml/1 tsp lemon juice in a heavy saucepan. Cook the mixture over low heat, stirring occasionally, until the berries have given off some liquid but still retain their shape, 5–7 minutes. Remove from the heat and set aside.

5 Place the pastry base in the oven and bake for 15 minutes. Remove and let cool while making the filling.

6 Beat together the cream cheese and remaining granulated sugar until light and fluffy. Add the egg, 15ml/1 tbsp lemon juice, the liqueur, if using, and the cream and beat until thoroughly blended.

7 Pour the cheese mixture into the pastry base and spread evenly. Bake until just set, 20–25 minutes.

8 Let the cheesecake cool completely on a wire rack, then cover and chill for at least 1 hour.

9 Spread the blueberry mixture evenly over the top of the cheesecake. Serve at cool room temperature.

> COOK'S TIP
>
> The cheesecake can be prepared 1 day in advance, but add the fruit shortly before serving.

Key Lime Pie

Key limes come from Florida but if they are not available, ordinary limes will do just as well.

Serves 8

3 large egg yolks

400g/14oz can sweetened condensed milk

15ml/1 tbsp grated Key lime rind

120ml/4fl oz/½ cup fresh Key lime juice

green food colouring (optional)

120ml/4fl oz/½ cup whipping cream

For the crust

1¼ cups digestive biscuit crumbs

75ml/5 tbsp butter or margarine, melted

1 Preheat the oven to 180°C/350°F/Gas 4. For the crust, place the biscuit crumbs in a bowl and add the butter or margarine. Mix to combine.

2 Press the crumbs evenly over the bottom and sides of a 23cm/9in pie dish or tin. Bake for 8 minutes. Let cool.

3 Beat the yolks until thick. Beat in the milk, lime rind and juice, and colouring, if using. Pour into the prebaked pie crust and refrigerate until set, about 4 hours. To serve, whip the cream. Pipe a lattice pattern on top, or spoon dollops around the edge.

Fruit Tartlets

The chocolate pastry cases make a dramatic base to these tartlets.

Makes 8

215g/7½oz/¾ cup redcurrant or grape jelly

15ml/1 tbsp fresh lemon juice

175ml/6fl oz/¾ cup whipping cream

675g/1½lb fresh fruit, such as strawberries, raspberries, kiwi fruit, peaches, grapes or blueberries, peeled and sliced as necessary

For the pastry

150g/5oz/⅔ cup cold butter, cut in pieces

65g/2½oz/⅓ cup dark brown sugar, firmly packed

45ml/3 tbsp unsweetened cocoa powder

175g/6oz/1½ cups plain flour

1 egg white

1 For the pastry, combine the butter, brown sugar and cocoa over low heat. When the butter is melted, remove from the heat and sift over the flour. Stir, then add just enough egg white to bind the mixture. Gather into a ball, wrap in greaseproof paper, and chill for at least 30 minutes.

2 Preheat the oven to 180°C/350°F/Gas 4. Grease eight 7.5cm/3in tartlet tins. Roll out the dough between two sheets of greaseproof paper and stamp out eight 10cm/4in rounds with a fluted cutter.

3 Line the tartlet tins with dough. Prick the bottoms. Chill for 15 minutes.

4 Bake until firm, 20–25 minutes. Leave to cool, then remove from the tins.

5 Melt the jelly with the lemon juice. Brush a thin layer in the bottom of the tartlets. Whip the cream and spread a thin layer in the tartlet shells. Arrange the fruit on top. Brush evenly with the glaze and serve.

Chocolate Chiffon Pie

This light and creamy dessert is as luxurious as its name suggests

INGREDIENTS

Serves 8

175g/6oz plain chocolate squares

25g/1oz square bitter chocolate

250ml/8fl oz/1 cup milk

15ml/1 tbsp gelatine, or alternative

130g/4½oz/⅔ cup granulated sugar

2 large eggs, separated

5ml/1 tsp vanilla essence

350ml/12fl oz/1½ cups whipping cream

pinch of salt

whipped cream and chocolate curls, to
   decorate

For the crust

75g/3oz/1½ cups digestive biscuit crumbs

75g/3oz/6 tbsp butter, melted

1 Place a baking sheet in the oven and preheat to 180°C/350°F/Gas 4. For the crust, mix the digestive biscuit crumbs and butter in a bowl. Press the crumbs evenly over the bottom and sides of a 23cm/9in pie tin. Bake for 8 minutes. Let cool.

2 Chop the chocolate, then grind in a food processor or blender. Set aside.

3 Place the milk in the top of a double boiler or in a heatproof bowl. Sprinkle over the gelatine. Let stand 5 minutes to soften.

4 Set the top of the double boiler or heatproof bowl over hot water. Add 50g/2oz/⅓ cup of the sugar, the chocolate and egg yolks. Stir until dissolved. Add the vanilla essence.

5 Set the top of the double boiler in a bowl of ice and stir until the mixture reaches room temperature. Remove from the ice and set aside.

6 Whip the cream lightly. Set aside. With an electric mixer, beat the egg whites and salt until they hold soft peaks. Add the remaining sugar and beat only enough to blend.

7 Fold a dollop of egg whites into the chocolate mixture, then pour back into the whites and gently fold in.

8 Fold in the whipped cream and pour into the pastry shell. Put in the freezer until just set, about 5 minutes. If the centre sinks, fill with any remaining mixture. Chill for 3–4 hours. Decorate with whipped cream and chocolate curls. Serve cold.

Coconut Cream Pie

Once you have made the pastry, the delicious filling can be put together in moments.

Serves 8

200g/7oz/2½ cups shredded coconut
115g/4oz/⅔ cup caster sugar
60ml/4 tbsp cornflour
pinch of salt
600ml/1 pint/2½ cups milk
50ml/2fl oz/¼ cup whipping cream
2 egg yolks
25g/1oz/2 tbsp unsalted butter
10ml/2 tsp vanilla essence

For the pastry

115g/4oz/1 cup plain flour
1.5ml/¼ tsp salt
40g/1½oz/3 tbsp cold butter, cut in pieces
25g/1oz/2 tbsp cold lard

1 For the pastry, sift the flour and salt into a bowl. Add the butter and lard and cut in with a pastry blender or two knives until the mixture resembles coarse breadcrumbs.

2 With a fork, stir in just enough iced water to bind the dough (30–45ml/2–3 tbsp). Gather into a ball, wrap in greaseproof paper and chill for at least 20 minutes.

3 Preheat the oven to 220°C/ 425°F/Gas 7. Roll out the dough 3mm/⅛in thick. Transfer to a 23cm/9in flan tin. Trim and flute the edges. Prick the bottom. Line with greaseproof paper and fill with baking beans. Bake for 10–12 minutes. Remove the paper and beans, reduce the heat to 180°C/350°F/Gas 4 and bake until brown, about 10–15 minutes more.

4 Spread 75g/3oz/1 cup of the coconut on a baking sheet and toast in the oven until golden, 6–8 minutes, stirring often. Set aside for decorating.

5 Put the sugar, cornflour and salt in a saucepan. In a bowl, whisk together the milk, cream and egg yolks. Add the egg mixture to the saucepan.

6 Cook over low heat, stirring constantly, until the mixture comes to the boil. Boil for 1 minute, then remove from the heat. Add the butter, vanilla essence and remaining coconut.

7 Pour into the pre-baked pastry case. When the filling is cool, sprinkle toasted coconut in a ring in the centre.

Cherry Pie

The woven lattice is the perfect finishing touch, although you can cheat and use a lattice pastry roller if you prefer.

Serves 8

900g/2lb fresh Morello cherries, stoned, or
   2 x 450g /1lb cans or jars, drained and
   stoned
65g/2½oz/generous ¾ cup caster sugar
25g/1oz/¼ cup plain flour
25ml/1½ tbsp fresh lemon juice
1.5ml/¼ tsp almond essence
25g/1oz/2 tbsp butter or margarine

For the pastry

225g/8oz/2 cups plain flour
5ml/1 tsp salt
175g/6oz/¾ cup lard or vegetable fat

1 For the pastry, sift the flour and salt into a mixing bowl. Using a pastry blender, cut in the fat until the mixture resembles coarse breadcrumbs.

2 Sprinkle in 60–75ml/4–5 tbsp iced water, a tablespoon at a time, tossing lightly with your fingertips or a fork until the pastry forms a ball.

3 Preheat the oven to 220°C/ 425°F/Gas 7. Divide the pastry in half and shape each half into a ball. On a lightly floured surface, roll out one of the balls to a circle about 30cm/12in in diameter.

4 Use it to line a 23cm/9in pie tin, easing the pastry in and being careful not to stretch it. With scissors, trim off excess pastry, leaving a 1cm/½in overhang around the pie tin.

5 Roll out the remaining pastry to 3mm/⅛in thick. Cut out eleven strips 1cm/½in wide.

6 In a mixing bowl, combine the cherries, sugar, flour, lemon juice and almond essence. Spoon the mixture into the pastry case and dot the top with the butter or margarine.

7 To make the lattice, place five of the pastry strips evenly across the filling. Fold every other strip back. Lay the first strip across in the opposite direction. Continue in this pattern, folding back every other strip each time you add a cross strip.

8 Trim the ends of the lattice strips even with the case overhang. Press together so that the edge rests on the pie-tin rim. With your thumbs, flute the edge. Chill for 15 minutes.

9 Bake the pie for 30 minutes, covering the edge of the pastry case with foil, if necessary, to prevent over-browning. Let cool, in the tin, on a wire rack.

Lemon Meringue Pie

Serve this exactly as it is, hot,
warm or cold. It doesn't need any
accompaniment.

INGREDIENTS

Serves 8
grated rind and juice of 1 large lemon
200g/7oz/1 cup caster sugar
25g/1oz/2 tbsp butter
45ml/3 tbsp cornflour
3 eggs, separated
pinch of salt
0.75ml/⅛ tsp cream of tartar

For the pastry
115g/4oz/1 cup plain flour
2.5ml/½ tsp salt
65g/2½oz/⅓ cup cold lard, cut into pieces

1 For the pastry, sift the flour and salt into a bowl. Add the lard and cut in with a pastry blender until the mixture resembles coarse crumbs. With a fork, stir in just enough iced water to bind the dough (about 30ml/ 2 tbsp). Gather the dough into a ball.

2 On a lightly floured surface, roll out the dough to 3mm/⅛in thick. Transfer to a 23cm/9in pie tin and trim the edge to leave a 1cm/½in overhang.

3 Fold the overhang under and crimp the edge. Chill the pie shell in the fridge for at least 20 minutes. Preheat the oven to 200°C/400°F/Gas 6.

4 Prick the dough all over with a fork. Line with greaseproof paper and fill with baking beans. Bake for 12 minutes. Remove the paper and beans and continue baking until golden, about 6–8 minutes more.

5 In a saucepan, combine the lemon rind and juice, 90g/ 3½oz/½ cup sugar, butter and 250ml/8fl oz/1 cup of water. Bring the mixture to the boil.

6 Meanwhile, in a mixing bowl, dissolve the cornflour in 15ml/1 tbsp cold water. Add the egg yolks.

7 Add the egg yolks to the lemon mixture and return to the boil, whisking continuously until the mixture thickens, about 5 minutes.

8 Cover the surface with grease-proof paper to prevent a skin forming and let cool.

9 For the meringue, using an electric mixer beat the egg whites with the salt and cream of tartar until they hold stiff peaks. Add the remaining sugar and beat until glossy.

10 Spoon the lemon mixture into the pie shell and spread level. Spoon the meringue on top, smoothing it up to the edge of the crust to seal. Bake until golden, 12–15 minutes.

Rich Chocolate-Berry Tart

Use any berries you like to top this exotic tart.

INGREDIENTS

Serves 10

115g/4oz/½ cup unsalted butter, softened

90g/3½oz/½ cup caster sugar

2.5ml/½ tsp salt

15ml/1 tbsp vanilla essence

50g/2oz/½ cup unsweetened cocoa

215g/7½oz/1¾ cups plain flour

450g/1lb fresh berries for topping

For the chocolate ganache filling

475ml/16fl oz/2 cups double cream

150g/5oz/½ cup seedless blackberry
preserve

225g/8oz plain chocolate, chopped

25g/1oz/2 tbsp unsalted butter

For the blackberry sauce

225g/8oz fresh or frozen blackberries
or raspberries

15ml/1 tbsp lemon juice

25g/1oz/2 tbsp caster sugar

30ml/2 tbsp blackberry liqueur

1 Prepare the pastry. Place the butter, sugar, salt and vanilla in a food processor and process until creamy. Add the cocoa and process for 1 minute. Add the flour all at once and process for 10–15 seconds, until just blended. Place a piece of clear film on a work surface. Turn out the dough on to the clear film. Use the film to help shape the dough into a flat disc and wrap tightly. Chill for 1 hour.

2 Lightly grease a 23cm/9in tart tin with a removable base. Roll out the dough between two sheets of clear film to a 28cm/11in round, about 5 mm/¼in thick. Peel off the top sheet of clear film and invert the dough into the prepared tin. Ease it in. Remove the clear film.

3 With floured fingers, press the dough on to the base and sides of the tin, then roll a rolling pin over the edge of the tin to cut off any excess dough. Prick the base with a fork. Chill for 1 hour. Preheat the oven to 180°C/ 350°F/Gas 4. Line the tart with foil or baking paper; fill with dry beans. Bake for 10 minutes; lift out the foil with the beans and bake for 5 minutes more, until just set (pastry may look underdone on the bottom, but will dry out). Remove to a wire rack to cool.

4 Prepare the filling. In a medium saucepan over medium heat, bring the cream and blackberry preserve to the boil. Remove from the heat and add the chocolate, stirring until smooth. Stir in the butter and strain into the cooled tart, smoothing the top. Cool the tart completely.

5 Prepare the sauce. In a food processor combine the blackberries, lemon juice and sugar and process until smooth. Strain into a bowl and add the liqueur. If it is too thick, thin with a little water.

6 To serve, remove the tart from the tin. Place on a serving plate and arrange the berries on top. With a pastry brush, brush with a little of the blackberry sauce to glaze lightly. Serve the remaining sauce separately.

Chocolate Pecan Torte

This torte uses finely ground nuts instead of flour. Toast then cool the nuts before grinding finely in a blender or food processor. Do not over-grind the nuts, as the oils will form a paste.

INGREDIENTS

Serves 16

200g/7oz bittersweet or plain chocolate, chopped

150g/5oz/10 tbsp unsalted butter, cut into pieces

4 eggs

90g/3½oz/½ cup caster sugar

10ml/2 tsp vanilla essence

115g/4oz/1 cup ground pecans

10ml/2 tsp ground cinnamon

24 toasted pecan halves, to decorate (optional)

For the chocolate honey glaze

115g/4oz bittersweet or semi-sweet chocolate, chopped

50g/2oz/¼ cup unsalted butter, cut into pieces

30ml/2 tbsp clear honey

pinch of ground cinnamon

1 Preheat the oven to 180°C/ 350°F/Gas 4. Grease a 20 x 5cm/8 x 2in springform tin; line with baking paper then grease the paper. Wrap the bottom and sides of the tin with foil to prevent water seeping in. In a saucepan over a low heat, melt the chocolate and butter, stirring until smooth. Remove from the heat. In a mixing bowl with an electric mixer, beat the eggs, sugar and vanilla essence until frothy, 1–2 minutes. Stir in the melted chocolate, ground nuts and cinnamon. Pour into the prepared tin.

2 Place the foil-wrapped tin in a large roasting tin and pour boiling water into the roasting tin, to come 2cm/¾in up the side of the springform tin. Bake for 25–30 minutes until the edge of the cake is set, but the centre is soft. Remove the tin from the water bath and remove the foil. Cool on a rack.

3 Prepare the glaze. In a small saucepan over low heat, melt the chocolate, butter, honey and cinnamon, stirring until smooth; remove from the heat. Carefully dip the toasted pecan halves halfway into the glaze and place on a non-stick baking paper-lined baking sheet until it is set.

4 Remove the sides from the tin and invert the cake on to a wire rack. Remove the tin bottom and paper, so the bottom of the cake is now the top. Pour the thickened glaze over the cake, tilting the rack slightly to spread the glaze. Use a metal palette knife to smooth the sides. Arrange the glazed nuts around outside edge of the torte and allow the glaze to set.

Peach Tart with Almond Cream

The almond cream filling should be baked until it is just turning brown. Take care not to overbake it or the delicate flavours will be spoilt.

Serves 8–10

4 large ripe peaches
115g/4oz/⅔ cup blanched almonds
30ml/2 tbsp plain flour
90g/3½oz/7 tbsp unsalted butter, at room
    temperature
130g/4½oz/scant ¾ cup granulated sugar
1 egg
1 egg yolk
2.5ml/½ tsp vanilla essence, or 10ml/
    2 tsp rum

For the pastry
150g/5oz/1¼ cups flour
4ml/¾ tsp salt
90g/3½oz/7 tbsp cold unsalted butter, cut
    in pieces
1 egg yolk

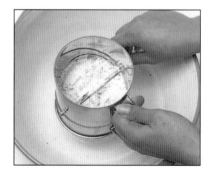

1 For the pastry, sift the flour and salt into a bowl.

2 Add the butter and cut in with a pastry blender until the mixture resembles coarse crumbs. With a fork, stir in the egg yolk and just enough iced water (30–45ml/ 2–3 tbsp) to bind the dough. Gather into a ball, wrap in grease-proof paper and chill for at least 20 minutes. Place a baking sheet in the oven and preheat to 200°C/400°F/Gas 6.

3 On a lightly floured surface, roll out the pastry 3mm/⅛in thick. Transfer to a 25cm/10in flan tin. Trim the edge, prick the bottom and chill.

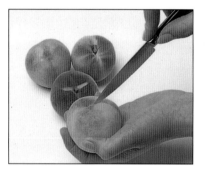

4 Score the bottoms of the peaches. Drop the peaches, one at a time, into boiling water. Leave for 20 seconds, then dip in cold water. Peel off the skins using a sharp knife.

5 Grind the almonds finely with the flour in a food processor, blender or nut grinder. With an electric mixer, cream the butter and 90g/3½oz/½ cup of the sugar until light and fluffy. Gradually beat in the egg and yolk. Stir in the almonds and vanilla or rum. Spread in the pastry shell.

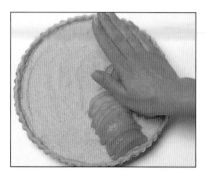

6 Halve the peaches and remove the stones. Cut crosswise in thin slices and arrange on top of the almond cream like the spokes of a wheel; keep the slices of each peach-half together. Fan them out by pressing down gently at a slight angle.

7 Bake until the pastry begins to brown, 10–15 minutes. Lower the heat to 180°C/350°F/Gas 4 and continue baking until the almond cream sets, about 15 minutes more. Ten minutes before the end of the cooking time, sprinkle with the remaining sugar.

VARIATION

For a Nectarine and Apricot Tart with Almond Cream, replace the peaches with nectarines, prepared and arranged the same way. Peel and chop three fresh apricots. Fill the spaces between the fanned-out nectarines with chopped apricots. Bake as above.

Index